FAMILY WALKS AND HIKES ON GREATER VANCOUVER'S NORTH SHORE

FAMILY WALKS AND HIKES ON GREATER VANCOUVER'S NORTH SHORE

HARRISON (HARRY) CRERAR

RMB

For information on purchasing bulk quantities of this book, or to obtain media excerpts or invite the author to speak at an event, please visit rmbooks.com and select the "Contact" tab.

RMB | Rocky Mountain Books Ltd.
rmbooks.com
@rmbooks
facebook.com/rmbooks

Cataloguing data available from Library and Archives Canada
ISBN 9781771604291 (paperback)
ISBN 9781771604307 (electronic)

All photographs are by the author unless otherwise noted.

Printed and bound in Canada

We would like to also take this opportunity to acknowledge the traditional territories upon which we live and work. In Calgary, Alberta, we acknowledge the Niitsitapi (Blackfoot) and the people of the Treaty 7 region in Southern Alberta, which includes the Siksika, the Piikuni, the Kainai, the Tsuut'ina and the Stoney Nakoda First Nations, including Chiniki, Bearpaw, and Wesley First Nations. The City of Calgary is also home to Métis Nation of Alberta, Region III. In Victoria, British Columbia, we acknowledge the traditional territories of the Lkwungen (Esquimalt, and Songhees), Malahat, Pacheedaht, Scia'new, T'Sou-ke and W̱SÁNEĆ (Pauquachin, Tsartlip, Tsawout, Tseycum) peoples.

We acknowledge the financial support of the Government of Canada through the Canada Book Fund and the Canada Council for the Arts, and of the province of British Columbia through the British Columbia Arts Council and the Book Publishing Tax Credit.

Disclaimer

The actions described in this book may be considered inherently dangerous activities. Individuals undertake these activities at their own risk. The information put forth in this guide has been collected from a variety of sources and is not guaranteed to be completely accurate or reliable. Many conditions and some information may change owing to weather and numerous other factors beyond the control of the authors and publishers. Individuals or groups must determine the risks, use their own judgment, and take full responsibility for their actions. Do not depend on any information found in this book for your own personal safety. Your safety depends on your own good judgment based on your skills, education, and experience.

It is up to the users of this guidebook to acquire the necessary skills for safe experiences and to exercise caution in potentially hazardous areas. The authors and publishers of this guide accept no responsibility for your actions or the results that occur from another's actions, choices, or judgments. If you have any doubt as to your safety or your ability to attempt anything described in this guidebook, do not attempt it.

CONTENTS

To my parents for introducing me to everything nature and hiking have to offer.

ABOUT FAMILY WALKS AND HIKES

At any age, completing a hike is an epic accomplishment for a kid. One of my earliest memories is climbing Goat Mountain (Hike 33) around the age of 5 with my father. After leaving the bustle of Grouse Mountain behind and venturing into the woods — stopping to eat mountain blueberries along the way — I scrambled up the last few metres of granite and reached the summit plateau, with its panoramic views of Vancouver and myriad bluffs and rocks to climb. It felt like I was on top of the world.

Hiking is a great activity for families. Siblings and parents can bond while exploring all that nature has to offer, leading to moments of discovery and exhilaration like my first Goat Mountain hike. Greater Vancouver's North Shore, with its unique blend of accessible wilderness, history and proximity to a major city, is the ideal place for a family adventure. It has everything from neighbourhood walks (such as Lower Capilano Pacific Trail, Hike 10) to easy seaside and lakeside strolls (Rice Lake, Hike 40) to rugged mountain adventures (Mount Seymour, Hike 50). Kids and families of all ages and fitness levels can find their ideal trail and destination.

Why hike with kids? At first, at any age, they're usually less than enthusiastic about the idea of leaving home and the lazy comfort of glowing screens to venture into unknown territory. Yet there are many rewards. Beyond the obvious sense of accomplishment, there's something on some hike, somewhere, for every kid. Explore beautiful waterfalls and burbling streams. Wonder at salmon, eagles and other wildlife. Scramble up (safe) rocky bluffs. Search for geocaches under rocks and stumps. The possibilities are literally endless.

Families can make hikes more enjoyable by turning them into an opportunity to explore together and bond with each other. For example, make hiking an Easter egg hunt by encouraging kids to find as many different mushrooms, rocks, trees and bugs as possible. Consider keeping a journal, or at least a checklist, after every hike. Another form of Easter egg hunt is geocaching, an activity where you use a GPS or smartphone to find hidden "treasures," usually a box with a logbook and small toys/keepsakes to exchange (download the Geocaching.com app for a list and map of North Shore geocaches). With younger kids, play games along the trail, such as I spy, tag, or hide-and-seek. If kids are getting tired, snacks (I recommend chocolate) seem to taste better on hikes, and will supply that much-needed last burst of energy. You might be surprised to find that your children want to come back to the same hike with friends or other family. They can now act as a tour guide, showing everyone the things they found the first time.

Happy hiking!

How the hikes were selected

The Greater Vancouver area has many, many hikes that might be interesting for kids. I've narrowed them down using the following criteria:

1. All hikes in this book are on the North Shore or Howe Sound islands. These hikes are the closest to the city of Vancouver (other than hikes in Stanley Park and the Endowment Lands, well documented in other books) and (mostly) accessible via public transit.

2. Every hike includes something interesting for children. Every child's interests are different, so I've highlighted what these interesting aspects are. For example, kindergarteners might enjoy the easy hikes to playgrounds at Cates Park (Hike 44) and Mackay Creek (Hike 25), while older kids can enjoy the views and scrambling at Mount Seymour (Hike 50). Some hikes have greater chances of seeing wildlife, such as salamanders at Mystery Lake (Hike 48), otters on the West Vancouver Waterfront (Hike 9) or eagles on the Coho Loop (Hike 23). Adventurous kids will like the water taxi ride to the Mount Artaban trailhead (Hike 12), or the "into-the-wild" feeling at Goat Ridge (Hike 34). Water of any kind — waterfalls, rivers or even lakes — is very interesting to kids, and many hikes feature water as the destination or along the trail.

Safety

Every parent (understandably) worries about safety, and hiking may seem like an inherently unsafe activity. This is not the case, especially somewhere like the North Shore with safe trails and few hazards. Statistically, the drive to the trailhead is much riskier than the actual hike, and nothing in life — even sitting at home browsing social media — is risk-free. That said, hikers should be aware of the following hazards.

Animals

Many people are understandably scared to encounter a bear or cougar on their hikes. Black bears, while rare, are the more common of the two by far (grizzly bears, which are much scarier, have not been sighted in the Vancouver area since they were driven to extinction in the early 1900s). Make some noise while hiking to avoid startling bears, especially on mountain hikes with lots of blueberries, such as Hollyburn Mountain and Mount Seymour (although most kids don't need to be told to make noise). Avoid letting dogs off leash in remote areas, as they sometimes harass or attract bears. If you see a bear, keep kids and dogs close, wave your arms to look scarier, and make more noise. Remember that the bear is probably more scared of you than you are scared of the bear. *Do not* turn your back or run. Realistically, you won't see a cougar: in my family's years of experience hiking and living on the North Shore, we've only seen one, and it was walking down a suburban street in Lynn Valley. If you see one, however, do the same as you would for a black bear: keep kids close, make noise and look bigger.

Navigation

It's hard to get lost on most trails in this book, but some of the mountain hikes might be trickier to navigate. I recommend carrying a GPS and/or map and compass.

Weather

Mountain weather can change quickly. It's a good idea to wear layers, bring rain gear (we do live in a rainforest, after all) and maybe bring a change of clothes. Also, rain makes surfaces much more slippery, so be more cautious when scrambling on rocks and hiking over logs. The appendix has a list of suggested hikes for rainy days.

Equipment

The hikes in this book vary widely and, as a result, so does the required equipment. A stroll along the Lonsdale Waterfront (Hike 29) will not need as much equipment as a hike to Kennedy Falls (Hike 35) or Mount Seymour (Hike 50). Consider wearing good footwear (either hiking boots or, on easier trails, comfortable trail runners). Lightweight equipment is expensive but makes a huge difference, especially on longer trails.

The Ten Essentials

The "Ten Essentials" are a list of items recommended for backcountry hiking (easier hikes in this book may not require all ten, especially hikes close to civilization).

1. Navigation (map or GPS): Always bring this. If you're relying on an app, bring a backup phone charger. Solar chargers may not work in our changeable mountain weather.

2. Water: Bring more water than you think you'll need, just in case.

3. Food: This is essential for any hike with kids. Consider bringing candy or another favourite snack to provide incentive or that all-important jolt of sugar to get them through the last kilometre. Endurance sports candies (such as Sport Beans) are useful.

4. Sun protection: Bring sunscreen, a hat and sunglasses.

5. Light (flashlight or headlamp): This is essential on any long hike. North Shore Rescue (NSR) has rescued many people caught in the backcountry after dark.

6. Weather-appropriate clothing and extra layers: North Shore weather, especially at higher altitudes, is highly changeable. Always prepare for rain.

7. First aid kit: Bring a kit with basic first aid equipment such as Band-Aids, wipes and antiseptic cream (e.g., Polysporin). There are many wilderness first aid kit checklists available online.

8. Fire starter and matches: Not needed for short city walks such as the Lonsdale waterfront.

9. Repair kit and tools (e.g., a pocketknife): Again, probably not needed for short city walks.

10. Emergency shelter: On backcountry hikes, some form of shelter (such as a tarp or space blanket) will be very helpful in a worst-case scenario, especially if it is raining or cold.

Difficulty

Every child is different, and everyone has different comfort zones, outdoor confidence and physical stamina. A high school athlete may be capable of longer hikes but less comfortable with heights or route finding in the wilderness. On the other hand, a younger child may like climbing and exploring but not have the stamina to go very far. Keeping this in mind, I gave each trail a rating out of 5, but I've also mentioned specific hazards and aspects of the trail that might pose difficulties. (Steep or flat? Rough or groomed trail? Long or short? Route finding needed?)

1. 1 out of 5: Very easy; these trails are flat, wheelchair- and stroller-accessible and short.

2. 2 out of 5: Easy; slightly longer or steeper than a 1 but still accessible to most children.

3. 3 out of 5: Moderate; these trails are two or more of the following: more than 5 km long, have steep sections and are above 200 m elevation.

4. 4 out of 5: Strenuous; these trails are either longer than 10 km, mostly uphill, route finding needed, risk of exposure, more than 400 m elevation gain or some of these combined.

5. 5 out of 5: Very strenuous; these trails are remote and have most or all criteria for a 4 rating.

Further adventures

There's always more to explore, especially with the North Shore's extensive trail network. For most hikes, I've identified possibilities for further exploration, such as trail extensions or connections to other hikes in the book. If these additions have a different difficulty rating than the rest of the hike (e.g., the Suicide Bluffs Trail is accessed from Dog Mountain but is more remote), it will be noted.

"Best of" lists

Can't decide? In the appendix at the back of the book, you'll find a series of lists for every occasion, from the best hikes in shoulder season or on a rainy day to the best beaches to the best adventures.

Camping

Being so close to civilization, most trails in this book don't lend themselves well to camping, or multiday hikes. However, some of the longer, more remote routes (especially in the mountains) are decent places to set up camp for the night: watching the sunrise or sunset from a mountain peak is definitely very memorable. A list of the best camping trips is included in the appendix. Note that camping is not allowed in some places (such as Bowen Island).

Public transit

Most hikes in this book are accessible via the North Shore's public transit system. Directions are provided except for the few hikes without transit access. Families considering a mountain hike via

Camping on Black Mountain. Courtesy David Crerar.

public transit should take bus route #236 (from Lonsdale Quay) or #232 (from Phibbs Exchange) to the Grouse Mountain Skyride and then take the Skyride to the top. The other trailheads for mountain hikes, Cypress Bowl and Mount Seymour, are not accessible by transit in hiking season.

A word on the Baden-Powell and Spirit trails

The Baden-Powell Trail, 48 km long, was built by Boy Scouts and Girl Guides in 1971 and named after the founder of the Scouting movement, Lord Robert Baden-Powell. It connects Horseshoe Bay and Deep Cove, passing over many highlights such as Black Mountain, the Cleveland Dam and the Lynn Canyon suspension bridge. Many North Shore hikes involve some part of the trail, including these hikes in the book:

1. Eagle Bluffs and Cougar Lake (Hike 19)

2. Black Mountain and Cabin Lake (Hike 18)

3. Yew Lake (Hike 20)

4. Mount Strachan (Hike 22)

5. Hollyburn Mountain (Hike 17)

6. Four Lakes Loop (Hike 16)

7. Lawson Creek Forestry Heritage Walk (Hike 7)

8. Brothers Creek Heritage Walk (Hike 8)

9. Cleveland Dam/Shinglebolt Trail (Hike 24)

10. Fisherman's Trail (Hike 42)

The more recent Spirit Trail is a less strenuous alternative to the Baden-Powell Trail. Begun in 2014, it is a paved pathway along the waterfront from Horseshoe Bay to Deep Cove. As of 2020, most of the trail is complete. In this book, the West Vancouver Waterfront (Hike 9), the Lower Capilano Pacific Trail (Hike 10), Lower Mackay Creek to Kings Mill Walk (Hike 26) and the Lonsdale Waterfront (Hike 29) are all or partly on the Spirit Trail.

West Vancouver

1. TUNNEL BLUFFS

*A challenging hike to a little-known viewpoint
hanging over Howe Sound.*

LOCATION

Park at Tunnel Point, 3.6 km north of Lions Bay and 1.3 km north of Brunswick Beach along the Sea to Sky Highway. (If you pass Porteau Cove, you've gone too far north.)

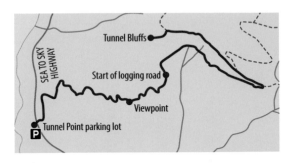

PUBLIC TRANSIT

None. The nearest bus stop is at Brunswick Beach, requiring a very dangerous 1.3-km hike along the highway.

DISTANCE

8-km round trip

ELEVATION GAIN

650 m

DIFFICULTY

Very strenuous (5). Very steep and slippery in places. The trailhead is across the highway from the parking lot. *Be very careful* when crossing the highway, for obvious reasons.

SEASON

Year-round

OF SPECIAL INTEREST FOR CHILDREN

This hike is more suitable for older children due to its steepness and sometimes rough trail, but the view at the end of the hike is an excellent reward for anyone who can make it. The old-growth forest at the start of the hike creates a nice atmosphere.

1. From the Tunnel Point parking lot, cross the Sea to Sky Highway. Be very careful; the crossing point is near a curve in the highway, creating a blind corner. The trailhead is marked with flagging tape.

2. Follow the yellow markers along a steep trail through old-growth arbutus forest. You will soon pass the first of many viewpoints, which make good rest stops, although the viewpoint at the end is much better.

3. The trail keeps climbing steadily uphill. Two sections have ropes to help you (be careful, and always assume any trail rope will break). Past the second rope, the trail reaches an old logging road and crosses small streams.

4. At a well-signed junction, go left (northwest) along another logging road (right leads to Mount Brunswick). At the next junction, turn left (northwest) again.

5. The trail ascends some more and then descends to the viewpoint. Enjoy the view of Howe Sound before returning the way you came.

A misty morning at Tunnel Bluffs. Courtesy David Crerar.

2. WHYTECLIFF PARK

This small park has many opportunities to explore, including the beach at Whytecliff Cove with lots of fun scrambling opportunities at low tide.

LOCATION
The park is located at the end of Marine Drive. From Highway 99, take exit #2 (Eagleridge Drive). Take the first exit at the round-about, turn left on Marine Drive, then continue to Whytecliff.

PUBLIC TRANSIT
The nearest bus stop is 2 km away from Tantalus Park (Marine Drive at Nelson Avenue), accessed by bus route #257 from downtown Vancouver and Park Royal. Continue along Marine Drive through a residential area to the park.

DISTANCE
0.6-km round trip (hike to beach and lookout); 1-km round trip (Panorama Ridge)

ELEVATION GAIN
13 m

DIFFICULTY
Easy (2).

SEASON
Year-round

OF SPECIAL INTEREST FOR CHILDREN
There is a beach and a good view of Howe Sound. At low tide, kids can walk to Whyte Islet, which is fun to explore, and they can look under rocks for marine life. There is also a playground and a field.

1. Beach and lookout:

- From the parking lot, a wide trail leads to Whytecliff Cove, a large rocky and sandy beach. Younger kids might enjoy looking for crabs under rocks. At low tide, you can walk over rocks to Whyte Islet, a relatively large island with some unofficial trails. You might see scuba divers — Whytecliff Park is apparently one of BC's best and most accessible diving sites.

- Hike west to a trail along the cliffs. A small beach is hidden between two cliffs and can be visited. The lookout at Whytecliff Point has an excellent view of Howe Sound.

- The loop returns to the parking lot.

2. Panorama Ridge:

- This section of the park is much less crowded. From the overflow parking lot, hike northeast along a narrow trail. There are several side trails to benches, although trees in front of most benches have grown and block the view.

- The trail ends at Hycroft Road, at the north end of the park.

Further Adventures

Batchelor Cove, a small rocky inlet, is just to the east of the park. There are two ways to access it, which can be combined to make a loop from the parking lot.

1. From the parking lot, walk or drive 400 m east along Marine Drive to a set of steps to Batchelor Cove.

2. From the northern end of the Panorama Ridge Trail, walk north along Hycroft Road. At a T-junction, turn left (north). There is a decent view of the Britannia Range. A short trail leads to Isleview Road. Turn right (southeast) on Isleview, walk uphill to join Copper Cove Road, turn right (west) on Marine Drive at a T-junction, then immediately turn left on Dufferin Avenue. Stairs at the end of Dufferin lead to Batchelor Cove.

3. WHYTE LAKE/NELSON CANYON

Follow a creek and canyon to a small,
peaceful mountain lake hidden above West Vancouver.

LOCATION

The trailhead is a small gravel parking lot on the north side of Westport Road (from Highway 99, take exit #4 to Westport Road). Check a map beforehand; the parking lot is a winding drive from the exit.

PUBLIC TRANSIT

None.

DISTANCE

5-km round trip

ELEVATION GAIN

160 m

DIFFICULTY

Moderate (3). Somewhat steep in areas. Passes near a canyon in some places, but the cliffs are easily avoidable.

SEASON

Usually snow-free year-round. Blackberries can be picked from late July to early September.

OF SPECIAL INTEREST FOR CHILDREN

The scenic, quiet lake with a dock and bench makes an ideal rest stop. Blackberries at the trailhead are an excellent pre- or post-hike snack when in season. There are several old-growth trees along the route. An abandoned highway bridge is a short detour west of the water tower. Owls can sometimes be seen at the lake. The west side of the lake has a lovely outhouse.

FACING PAGE FROM TOP Pippa, Isla and Angus at the Whyte Lake dock. Courtesy David Crerar; Whyte Lake. Courtesy David Crerar.

14

1. From the parking lot, hike west past blackberry bushes along a gravel road. The road passes under the highway bridge, enters Nelson Canyon Park and begins to climb. This is the steepest part of your journey.

2. You will soon reach a water tower. The road turns left here; heading left (northwest) for about 50 m takes you to an abandoned old highway bridge. Once you're done at the bridge, retrace your steps, leave the road, head uphill (to the northeast on the Trans Canada Trail) and climb some more.

3. At a Y-junction, turn left onto the Whyte Lake Trail. The trail turns left (downhill) and travels along the canyon rim. You will see several old-growth Douglas firs.

4. The trail crosses Nelson Creek via a wooden bridge. Later, cross Nelson Creek again then turn right.

5. You will soon reach Whyte Lake and its dock, to the north (right).

Further Adventures
The trail to the west (left) leads to the site of an old cabin and then travels along a boardwalk to a T-junction. Turn right (northeast), then right again at the next Y-junction to reach a small dirt beach with views of the dock. (The left turn at each junction connects to the Baden-Powell Trail). Along the way, you will pass a scenic outhouse.

4. KLOOTCHMAN PARK

This smaller, less crowded alternative to Lighthouse Park offers a short, steep hike to a clifftop ocean viewpoint.

LOCATION
The trailhead is at the end of Klootchman Walk. From Marine Drive, turn west on Howe Sound Lane. Keep following Howe Sound Lane downhill to a small parking area near its end.

PUBLIC TRANSIT
The closest bus stop is Marine Drive at the Crossway, serviced by route #250. From the bus stop, go west on the Crossway then turn right (west) on Howe Sound Lane.

DISTANCE
0.8-km round trip

ELEVATION GAIN
37 m

DIFFICULTY
Easy (2). The hike is relatively easy and short, but it is mostly downhill via stairs, and cliffs at the overlook must be avoided.

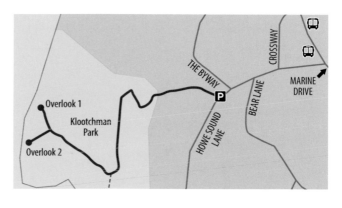

SEASON
Year-round

OF SPECIAL INTEREST FOR CHILDREN
Kids will enjoy the view of the ocean and arbutus trees. The solitude here is also a perk for older children.

1. From the parking lot, hike downhill through hemlock, cedar and arbutus trees. There is one wooden staircase and several

natural (root or stone) staircases. Kids may be interested in the peeling bark of the arbutus trees.

2. The trail forks near the end, leading to different viewpoints.

3. At the end of the trail, you will reach a rocky bluff with excellent views of Howe Sound. Keep young children away from the cliffs.

4. Return the way you came.

5. LIGHTHOUSE PARK

A large park with many excellent trails and beaches to explore beyond the famous lighthouse.

LOCATION
Travel west on Marine Drive through West Vancouver past scenic ocean views and beachfront mansions. Turn left on Beacon Lane and arrive at the parking lot after 300 m.

PUBLIC TRANSIT
Bus route #250 (Horseshoe Bay) stops at Marine and Beacon.

DISTANCE
The suggested route is 5 km, but there are over 10 km of side trails to explore. The direct route to the lighthouse is a 2-km round trip.

ELEVATION GAIN
Variable

DIFFICULTY
Moderate (3). Some trails are slightly rocky or steep. In some areas, some route finding may be needed to navigate the park's maze of side trails.

SEASON
Year-round

OF SPECIAL INTEREST FOR CHILDREN
The park's various side trails are a paradise

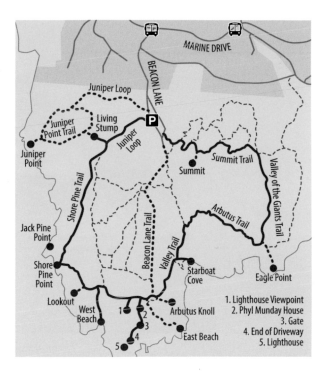

1. Lighthouse Viewpoint
2. Phyl Munday House
3. Gate
4. End of Driveway
5. Lighthouse

Point Atkinson Lighthouse stands sentinel over Burrard Inlet.

for adventurous children. Interesting destinations include the beaches at West Beach, Starboat Cove (and its old boat), and East Beach; views of the city at these beaches; tidepooling and searching for crabs; the lighthouse viewpoint and scrambling on rocks (especially at West Beach). This route takes you past most of the park's highlights.

1. From the parking lot, pick up a trail map at the information kiosk (located to the west, about halfway up the parking lot, the middle of three trailheads). Hike southwest on the Juniper Loop, passing an outhouse.

2. The trail reaches a Y-junction. Several metres up the trail to your right (west) is a living stump, still covered in bark. (A poster at the parking lot information kiosk explains that its roots have grafted to the next tree's roots, keeping it alive.) Please avoid climbing either tree. Retrace your steps to the main trail (or keep going along the Juniper Loop, which adds another 1 km; the trail leads to a rocky bluff above Howe Sound before returning to the parking lot via a boardwalk.)

3. Head south (downhill) on the Shore Pine Trail. You will pass a nurse log (a sign explains how these old fallen trees provide nutrition to growing plants). After about 400 m from the living stump, a short side trail leads to Shore Pine Point, a rocky bluff above a rocky, seaweed-covered beach. Keep kids safe on the bluff. Continuing on the Shore Pine Trail, another right turn leads to a lookout with a good view. Watch out for the maze of trails behind the lookout.

4. Return to the Shore Pine Trail. In several metres, turn right on the West Beach Trail. This slightly steep and rooty trail leads to a small rocky beach with lots of driftwood and a view of the lighthouse. Bluffs to your right (north) are fun to scramble on. When you're done, return to the Shore Pine Trail.

5. You will reach a Y-junction; stay east on the Shore Pine Trail and go right. Left leads to the Seven Sisters Trail, with a turnoff to Songbird and Salmonberry meadows. There used to be an

old outdoor theatre with benches in Songbird Meadow, which was fun to explore, but it was removed sometime after 2015.

6. The Shore Pine Trail leads to another right turn at the lighthouse viewpoint. A plaque on a cairn explains the lighthouse's history. Several trees block the view of the lighthouse. For a better view, keep going along the Shore Pine Trail then turn right at the cabin (originally an army hut during the Second World War, it is now the Phyl Munday Nature House, operated by the West Vancouver Girl Guides). If you're lucky, the gate to the lighthouse road will be open, and you can walk to the end of the driveway.

7. Once you're done, head back uphill along the road, turning right on the Valley Trail. You will see a sign for the East Beach Trail, leading to a rocky beach with an excellent view of the city and some rocks to scramble on. Explore here if you want.

8. Return to the Valley Trail and hike northeast. A right turn (marked with an 11) leads to Arbutus Knoll, with a decent view of the city and a picnic area, another nice place for a break.

9. Back on the Valley Trail, an easily missed right (southeast) leads to Starboat Cove, a peaceful rocky beach with a good city view and an abandoned metal boat. A side trail leads to a bench on a cliff to the southwest with a good view of the beach.

10. The Valley Trail reaches a Y-junction. Turn right (east) on the Arbutus Trail. After 300 m, you can turn right again on the Arbutus Trail, then right again to Eagle Point for a view. Otherwise, turn left (north) on the Valley of the Giants Trail.

11. This part of the park is less crowded on weekends. The Valley of the Giants Trail heads north through some old-growth forest before joining the Arbutus Trail. Any trails from here will lead to the parking lot. The Summit Trail goes via the park's high point, a bluff with no views. You might see fire hydrants along the way, which are used for forest fire protection.

FACING PAGE FROM TOP West Beach; Looking down on Starboat Cove.

6. CYPRESS FALLS

Another hidden gem with scenic waterfall and creek views, and some of the best old-growth forest left on the North Shore.

LOCATION
There are multiple access points, but this route starts from the Cypress Falls parking lot. From Highway 99, take exit #4 (Westport Road). Immediately after leaving the highway, turn right on Woodgreen Drive. Take the third right turn (Woodgreen Place; the names of the two preceding roads also begin with the word "wood," so be careful). The road curves past the tennis court parking lot to the trailhead.

PUBLIC TRANSIT
Woodgreen Drive at Woodgreen Place, accessible via bus route #250 (from Park Royal). From either bus stop (north- or southbound, walk to the end of Woodgreen Place).

DISTANCE
1-km round trip to lower falls; 3-km round trip to upper falls

ELEVATION GAIN
130 m

DIFFICULTY
Moderate (3) to lower falls; strenuous (4) to upper falls. Short but steep and rocky in areas. Some parts of the trail are very close to the canyon rim, especially near the upper falls. Few

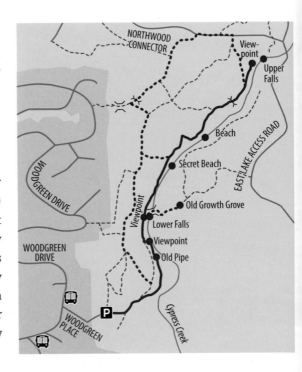

Angus discovers the remains of a wooden water pipe.

One of many old-growth trees to hug.

trails are marked and some route finding is needed, especially near the upper falls.

SEASON
Usually snow-free year-round.

OF SPECIAL INTEREST FOR CHILDREN
This hike has waterfalls and big old-growth trees, the latter among the best on the North Shore. The creek is also easily accessible in some areas, including at a "secret" small rocky beach (summer only); children can enjoy rock hopping and exploring, or just cooling down on a hot summer day. Also to be found are the ruins of an old wooden water pipe.

1. From the parking lot, hike past several thimbleberry bushes (delicious) into the forest. Immediately, you will turn left, uphill, onto the main trail. After 100 m, turn right onto a smaller trail that follows the canyon rim.

2. Along this trail, you will see coiled wire buried in the ground with old wood inside it. This was part of the old wooden water pipe system, built in the early 1900s to carry water from the mountains to West Vancouver and Vancouver. At 0.3 km,

Cooling off at Cypress Creek on a hot summer day.

there is a large tangled mass of wire left over from one of these pipes. Around this point, you will begin to see Lower Cypress Falls through the trees.

3. This side trail ends at a wooden railing at 0.4 km with a good view of the falls and canyon. You can scramble up the hill near the fence to rejoin the main trail, or backtrack a few metres to a much less steep scramble.

4. The main trail descends for a few metres and then ascends to another fenced-off falls viewpoint at 0.5 km, this time above the falls.

5. Once you are done at the lower falls, keep going along the main trail past a wooden bridge (don't cross it) up a steep hill. (If this hill is too steep, or you thought the lower trail was too close to the canyon rim for comfort, see **Further Adventures #1** for a safer detour.) You will see several large old-growth trees — the first of many. The lack of clear marking in this area has created a maze of side trails leading all over the nearby hill. However, our route is marked by orange dia-mond-shaped markers on trees. Follow these markers uphill

and along the canyon rim through a grove of old-growth trees and past a small wooden bridge.

6. After this grove, a very steep short trail to the east leads to the creek. In the summer you can rock hop from here and explore the creek. Several metres upstream you will find a very small secret rocky beach. After returning to the main trail, a less steep and more obvious trail leads to another, larger rocky beach with rock-hopping opportunities. Both are great places to cool off on a hot day.

7. Keep travelling upstream, following the orange markers and staying well away from the canyon rim. The trail passes through a gate with a warning sign: you are entering the property of British Pacific Properties, which allows hikers to use the trail.

8. You will reach the end of the trail, with a good view of the upper falls through the trees. Keep small children away from the rim. Do not take the trail on your right (east) into the canyon; it's very steep and dangerous, and the view from the viewing area is much better anyway.

9. Return the way you came.

Further Adventures #1
If the upper falls trail seems too risky, this alternate trail is longer and less interesting but safer.

1. About 150 m before the wooden bridge over Cypress Creek, turn left (west) up a series of wooden steps to a trail marked by yellow markers and orange flagging tape. Alternatively, about 150 m past this bridge, turn left (west) up a connector and turn right (northeast) to join this trail.

2. Keep following the yellow markers and orange flagging tape up wood stairs and a rocky hill. You will reach a junction with a wooden bridge to your left (west) and a gate to your right (north). Turn right immediately before the bridge (crossing the bridge leads to a park at Woodgreen Drive).

FROM LEFT The gate guarding the upper falls; The upper waterfall is visible across its ravine.

3. Continue along this trail, ignoring side trails, until you reach a well-defined gravel road with a power line. Keep going uphill (north) on the gravel road, turning right after about 100 m onto a wide trail paved with bark mulch. This trail leads to the upper falls.

Further Adventures #2

A grove of old-growth trees can be found on the other side of the wooden bridge (see step 5) if the kids still have some energy.

1. Cross the bridge and hike up a steep hill; the trail flattens out right before the grove. If you reach a Y-junction, turn around: you've gone too far. (The left fork at this junction leads to a very dangerous and slippery trail along the canyon rim to an area above the upper falls, which provides absolutely no view. Turning right leads to the Eagle Lake access road. Either way, it's not worth it to keep going.)

7. LAWSON CREEK FORESTRY HERITAGE WALK

This guided loop trail explores the history of logging in West Vancouver by visiting historical sites and old-growth trees the loggers left behind. Note: Be sure to bring a copy of the brochure, available online at westvancouver.ca, to appreciate the history of the area.

LOCATION
The trail starts at the sign marked "Lawson Creek Forestry Heritage Walk" at the bridge near the intersection of Pinecrest Drive and Finch Hill in the British Properties. Drive north on Taylor Way and turn left on Southborough Drive, left again on Highland Drive, then left again on Eyremount Drive. Continue along Eyremount (which becomes Chartwell), and then turn right on Pinecrest Drive.

PUBLIC TRANSIT
The closest bus stop is Chartwell Drive at Sandhurst Place, accessed via bus route #254 from Park Royal. Hike up Chartwell and turn left on Pinecrest after 1 km.

DISTANCE
4.7-km loop

ELEVATION GAIN
300 m

DIFFICULTY
Moderate (3). A good-quality trail with some elevation gain.

SEASON
Usually snow-free year-round.

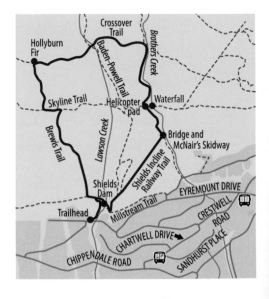

OF SPECIAL INTEREST FOR CHILDREN

The trail features many remnants of the logging industry, including an old dam, ruins of railways and corduroy roads, which will be interesting to imaginative kids. Make a scavenger hunt of the trip. These artifacts are a good way for kids to learn about and interact with West Vancouver history. Numbered stops correspond to the brochure. An old-growth Douglas fir (the Hollyburn Fir) and a waterfall are also interesting. A BC Hydro helicopter pad makes a good picnic spot.

1. Hike upstream on the west side of Lawson Creek. Within 100 m, you will see Shields Dam, built in 1917 to store shinglebolts (blocks of cedar to be cut into shingles). Below the dam, a log flume (water-filled wooden channel — no longer standing) carried shinglebolts to a mill 2 km downhill. (A reconstructed flume is visible at Rice Lake, Hike 40.)

2. Continue to the Millstream Trail, turn right (east), cross the creek and then turn left (northeast) onto a gravel road. After another 175 m, turn right (northeast) onto the Shields Incline Railway Trail, following the route of a railway carrying shinglebolts downhill. Keep an eye out for railway ties and spikes.

3. At the ruins of an old bridge, turn left (north). You will see a trench (McNair's Skidway), used to bring logs downhill. Near the power line 250 m ahead there is a waterfall worth visiting, and a helicopter pad (good for picnics). Continue uphill past the power line, following Brothers Creek, then turn left (west) on the Crossover Trail. You will cross the Baden-Powell Trail, Lawson Creek and Lawson Creek West before reaching the Hollyburn Fir, an 1,100-year-old Douglas fir almost 3 m in diameter.

4. Past the fir, turn left (south) on the Brewis Trail, left (east) on the Skyline Trail at the power lines then right (south) on the Brewis Trail after 100 m. After 1 km, turn left (east) on the Millstream Trail to rejoin the Shields Dam Trail and return to Pinecrest.

Further Adventures #1

Several trails connect to the Brothers Creek Heritage Walk (Hike 8).
I suggest turning right (east) at the helicopter pad and continuing to
the Candelabra Tree.

Further Adventures #2

If you continue uphill along the Baden-Powell Trail for 1.5 km past the
Crossover Trail turnoff, you will reach the junction to Blue Gentian
Lake (part of Hike 16). At the junction, turn left (west) to go to Blue
Gentian Lake, or north (straight) to go to Lost Lake.

ABOVE Shields Dam on a rainy afternoon. Courtesy David Crerar.
FACING PAGE Isla is ready to explore Brothers Creek. Courtesy David Crerar.

Caution!
Drop
Off

Brothers
Creek

District of
West Vancouver
Parks + Recreation

Lawson Creek
Forestry
Heritage Walk

← 3

33

8. BROTHERS CREEK HERITAGE WALK

*Another guided trail through West Vancouver's logging history.
Like the Lawson Creek Forestry Heritage Walk, the brochure
(available at westvancouver.ca) is a very useful guide.*

LOCATION
The trail starts at a gate marked "Brothers Creek Fire Road" next
to 1121 Millstream Road, 100 m east of the intersection of Millstream Road and Henlow Road. From the Upper Levels Highway,
take exit #11 (15th Street) and drive up Chartwell to Millstream.

PUBLIC TRANSIT
The closest bus stop is Eyremount Drive at Crestline Place, accessed
via route #254 from Park Royal. Hike up Crestline Road, turn left
on Henlow Road and then right on Millstream Road.

DISTANCE
6-km loop

ELEVATION GAIN
280 m

DIFFICULTY
Moderate (3).
Good trail with
some elevation
gain and steep
sections.

SEASON
Usually snow-free
year-round.

OF SPECIAL INTER-
EST FOR CHILDREN
Like the Lawson
Creek Forestry
Heritage Walk, this

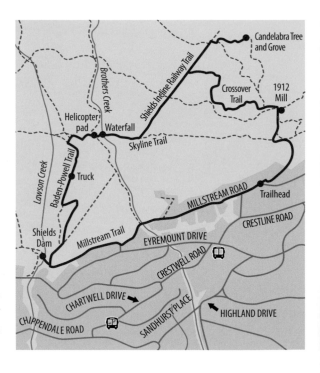

trail has many ruins from logging days (such as an old mill and steam donkey), which are fun to discover. There are also several old-growth trees, a helicopter pad and a waterfall.

1. Hike uphill past the gate. There are many large stumps, victims of logging in the early 1900s. Many were burned in a 1916 fire. Several parallel logs remain along the trail. Between 1908 and 1913, they supported a steam locomotive known as the "Walking Dudley." Turn left (west) on the Skyline Trail, then right (north). You will pass the ruins of a 1912 mill and a steam donkey (a steam-powered winch used to drag logs).

2. Turn left (west) again on the Crossover Trail, then right (north) on the fire road. Turn right (northeast) at a Y-junction with the Shields Incline Railway Trail, following the route of a railway that carried shinglebolts.

3. At the next switchback, leave the fire road and hike east. Descend to see the Candelabra, a dead Douglas fir (snag) shaped like a pitchfork. The trail continues downhill past several other snags to a living old-growth Douglas fir (2.7 m in diameter, 42.7 m tall).

4. Turn around and hike downhill on the Shields Incline Railway Trail to the junction with the Skyline Trail (just before the power line).

5. Head right (east) along the Skyline Trail, passing a viewpoint, a helicopter pad and Brothers Creek Falls. Here the trail intersects the Lawson Creek Forestry Heritage Walk (Hike 7).

6. Continue along the Skyline Trail past Brothers Creek Falls. Turn right (south) on the Baden-Powell Trail, passing the remains of a war surplus army truck.

7. Rejoin the Shields Incline Railway Trail and then turn right (west) on Millstream Trail to Shields Dam, built in 1917 to store shinglebolts (a block of cedar to be cut into shingles). Below the dam, a log flume (water-filled wooden channel — no longer standing) carried shinglebolts to a mill 2 km downhill.

FROM LEFT Brothers Creek Falls is visible from this wooden bridge downstream. Courtesy David Crerar; The remains of a truck. Courtesy David Crerar.

8. Turn around and hike east on the Millstream Trail to Millstream Road. The trailhead is 1 km to your left (east).

Further Adventures

If you continue uphill along the Baden-Powell Trail for 2 km past the power line, you will reach the junction to Blue Gentian Lake (Hike 16). At the junction, turn left (west) to go to Blue Gentian Lake, or north (straight) to go to Lost Lake.

9. WEST VANCOUVER WATERFRONT

An easy walk along the shores of Burrard Inlet.
There are many access points; hike for as long as you want.
Note: Dogs are only allowed on this route from 19th to 24th
streets and in the dog park at Ambleside.

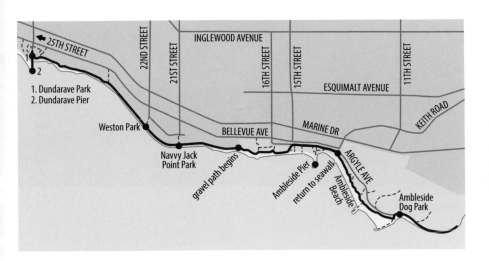

LOCATION
This route starts from the Dundarave Beach parking lot at the foot of 25th Street. However, there are many access points along the walk.

PUBLIC TRANSIT
The closest bus stop is 25th and Marine (accessed via buses #250, 251, 252, 253 and 255).

DISTANCE
3.4-km round trip to 18th Street; 7.6-km round trip to Park Royal

ELEVATION GAIN
None

DIFFICULTY
Very easy (1). Flat; suitable for strollers.

Otters swimming in McDonald Creek.

SEASON
Year-round

OF SPECIAL INTEREST FOR CHILDREN
Ambleside and Dundarave beaches are obvious destinations, with playgrounds at both for younger children. Wildlife, such as otters and herons, can often be found between Dundarave and Ambleside (especially during salmon spawning season in the fall). There are also several informational displays about local history (skilled storytellers can make these interesting to kids).

1. From Dundarave parking lot, hike to the Dundarave Pier. You can walk to the end of the pier if you like for a view of the seawall, West Vancouver, and the Lions Gate Bridge.

2. The path between Dundarave and 18th Street is officially known as the West Vancouver Centennial Seawalk. Hike east (toward the Lions Gate Bridge) along this walk. Keep an eye out for otters on the rocks to your right. You will pass Weston

FROM LEFT A grumpy otter on a foggy March morning; An otter and its prey.

Park and Navvy Jack Point Park, both of which have good benches for otter- or birdwatching.

3. At 18th Street, you leave the paved trail and the officially designated seawalk. Keep hiking along the shoreline on a gravel path.

4. The gravel path eventually ends. Side trails to your left lead to the Spirit Trail along Argyle Avenue. Continue along the Spirit Trail east. A short detour to your right leads to Ambleside Pier.

5. Past the Hollyburn Sailing Club, leave the Spirit Trail and hike along a seawall, which becomes the Capilano Pacific Trail (Hike 10) at another junction with the Spirit Trail at the eastern end of Ambleside Park. Park Royal is 200 m away.

10. LOWER CAPILANO PACIFIC TRAIL (AMBLESIDE TO WOODCROFT)

This trail follows the Capilano River through forest interrupted by suburbia. Hike upstream for as long as you want.

LOCATION

This trail starts at the Ambleside dog park (behind the golf course). Park near the end of Argyle Avenue. You can also join the trail at Park Royal.

PUBLIC TRANSIT

Marine Drive at 11th Street, accessed by buses #250, 251, 252, 253, 254, 255 and 256.

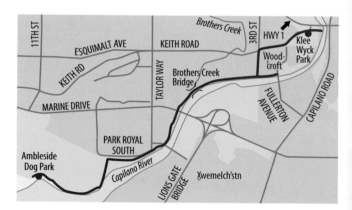

DISTANCE

4.6-km round trip to Woodcroft; 5.8-km round trip to Klee Wyck; 13.2-km round trip to Cleveland Dam (see **Further Adventures**)

ELEVATION GAIN

Minimal to Woodcroft; 158 m to Cleveland Dam

DIFFICULTY

Easy (2). Flat, wide, gravel trail. If continuing to Klee Wyck Park, the river access is very steep.

SEASON

Year-round. Salmon can be seen in Brothers Creek during spawning season (fall), and eagles can be seen trying to catch them.

A hungry eagle looking for salmon near Taylor Way.

OF SPECIAL INTEREST FOR CHILDREN

The trail has river views; when the river is low (for most of the summer and fall), kids can scramble down to the river in places and explore the riverbank. Wildlife can be seen, especially during spawning season. For many, Park Royal shopping mall and its many food options will also be a highlight. The hike starts and ends at Ambleside Park, another highlight.

1. From Ambleside, hike east along the seawall, which curves northward to follow the Capilano River. After passing under a railway bridge, the trail leads inland to Park Royal. The land in this area is part of X̱wemelch'stn (Homulchesan), a Squamish Nation reserve including Park Royal South and the community across the river. An info board near Taylor Way provides information about the Squamish people. Many eagles can be seen in the trees near the water during salmon spawning season (fall).

2. Continue under two bridges (Taylor Way and Marine Drive). Past Marine Drive, the trail enters the forest. A bridge crosses the mouth of Brothers Creek. In autumn, look down to find salmon in the pool under the bridge.

3. Keep hiking along the river. In some areas, you can scramble along the riverbank when the water level is low. The main Capilano Pacific Trail heads uphill 2.2 km from Ambleside, but a branch keeps going along the river for another 0.1 km before reaching the Woodcroft apartment complex on Fullerton Avenue. A rough trail continues under the Fullerton Avenue bridge before petering out 0.1 km later.

4. Return the way you came (or keep hiking; see **Further Adventures**).

Further Adventures #1

The trail continues to Klee Wyck Park.

1. Just before Woodcroft, turn left (uphill). The trail leads around Woodcroft to Keith Road.

2. Hike east (right) on Keith Road for 400 m to Klee Wyck Park.

Graffiti at Klee Wyck Park.

> **Historical Note** The house at Klee Wyck (named after the Haida name of artist Emily Carr, a friend of the owner's) was built in 1925. It was donated to West Vancouver in 1960, and was used as an arts centre before falling into disrepair.

3. Several metres past Klee Wyck, a sign indicates the Capilano Pacific Trail to the left. A faint, steep trail past this sign leads downhill to the Capilano River right below the highway bridge. Try to find a face, painted on concrete, hidden in the bushes. An island in the middle of the river is accessible when the water level is low.

Further Adventures #2
Keep hiking uphill to the Shinglebolt Trail (Hike 24), following the signs for the Capilano Pacific Trail. The trail ends at Cleveland Dam, 6.6 km from Ambleside.

Howe Sound Islands

11. MOUNT KILLAM

*An adventurous hike to a little-travelled corner of
Gambier Island with an excellent viewpoint overlooking
Howe Sound and Greater Vancouver.*

LOCATION

This hike starts from the dock at New Brighton, on the west
coast of Gambier Island. To access New Brighton, take the ferry
to Langdale on the Sunshine Coast and then take the BC Ferries
water taxi (foot passengers only) to New Brighton. Check the BC
Ferries website for schedules; sometimes the ferry stops at Keats
Island before visiting Gambier. You can also access New Brighton
via private boat, chartered water taxi or kayak.

PUBLIC TRANSIT

Horseshoe Bay is accessed by
bus routes #250 (via Dundarave) and 257 (express) from
downtown Vancouver. Sun-
shine Coast bus routes #1 and
90 stop at the Langdale ferry
terminal (check bctransit.com).

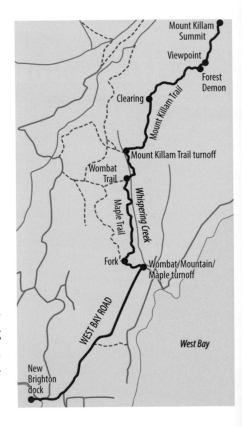

DISTANCE

12-km round trip to viewpoint;
13.2-km round trip to true
summit

ELEVATION GAIN

844 m

DIFFICULTY

Very strenuous (5). Route finding is needed on the logging
roads near the start. After that,
the climb is steep and sometimes slippery.

SEASON

Snow-free year-round.

OF SPECIAL INTEREST FOR CHILDREN

The water taxi will be fun for kids and adds to the adventure. There is a great view of Howe Sound from the viewpoint. There is a forest demon (actually, an interestingly shaped stump) guarding the trail. There are mossy meadows along the way.

As you approach Gambier Island on the water taxi from Langdale, look north toward the island. The two peaks on the island in front of you are Mount Killam (right/east) and Mount Liddell (left/west).

> **Historical Note** Mount Killam and Mount Liddell were named after David Killam and John Liddell, respectively. They both grew up in Vancouver and spent summers on Gambier Island, before dying in the Second World War.

1. From New Brighton, walk straight ahead (east) on the dirt road (West Bay Road). The road curves to the northeast and heads uphill. This is the start of the east route up Killam. (Most online write-ups describe a different route — the west route — involving a left turn at New Brighton. That route passes active logging areas, and it's easy to get lost in the maze of logging roads, especially if signs have been removed. The newer, east route is easier to follow and involves fewer gravel roads.)

2. Two kilometres past New Brighton, West Bay road does a 90-degree turn to the right (east). The trailhead is on your left (west), next to a driveway. The trail starts out as a combination of the Wombat, Mountain and Maple trails, each marked with their respective symbols. Keep right at two forks, following the Maple Trail. Past the second fork, Maple Trail dips downhill for a while before continuing uphill.

3. Maple Trail rejoins Wombat Trail a little over 1 km later. Go right (east) and cross Whispering Creek, then head left and uphill (north) on an old logging road.

4. In a few hundred metres, turn right on Mount Killam trail, which is flagged but easy to miss. If you cross Whispering Creek again, you've gone about 50 m too far.

5. Continue north and uphill. The trail gets steeper but is well flagged. You will pass a large mossy clearing where small wild raspberries can sometimes be found.

6. Near the top, at the base of a small cliff, a forest demon guards the peak. It sometimes wears sunglasses. This is a good example of a living stump; its roots have grafted to the next tree's roots, keeping it alive.

7. Around the 700-m level, a trail to your right (east) leads to the highlight of the hike: a viewpoint overlooking the many bays and peninsulas of southern Gambier Island, with Bowen Island, Greater Vancouver and Vancouver Island in the distance. This is a good place to have lunch. On sunny summer days, many boats can be seen sailing through Howe Sound.

8. If you'd like to keep going to the true peak, continue north along the ridge for half an hour. The summit is marked with a cairn. There are no views.

9. Return the way you came.

FACING PAGE FROM TOP Beware forest demons; The view from the Mount Killam viewpoint.

12. MOUNT ARTABAN

This mountain on Gambier Island, only accessible by boat,
offers good views of Howe Sound.

LOCATION
The trail starts at either Halkett Bay or Camp Fircom, both on the southeastern coast of Gambier Island. You'll need a water taxi, private boat or kayak to access either location. Water taxi companies include Cormorant Marine (www.cormorantwatertaxi.com; 604-250-2630) and Mercury Transport (www.mercurytransport.ca; 604-921-7451; scheduled stops at Fircom). All water taxis leave from Horseshoe Bay. Be sure to organize the trip in advance.

PUBLIC TRANSIT
Horseshoe Bay is accessed by bus routes #250 and 257 from downtown.

DISTANCE
8-km round trip from Camp Fircom; 10-km round trip from Halkett Bay

ELEVATION GAIN
615 m

DIFFICULTY
Strenuous (4). The trail is well marked but steep in some areas.

SEASON
Snow-free year-round. There are more scheduled water taxis during the summer.

OF SPECIAL INTEREST FOR CHILDREN

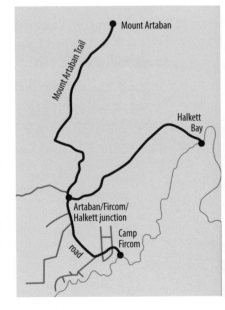

There are good views, and the water taxi will be fun for kids and adds to the adventure. Tree frogs can sometimes be heard along the trail.

1. From the dock at Camp Fircom, travel northeast along a gravel road to a junction with signs for Camp Fircom, Halkett Bay (straight ahead to the northeast) and Mount Artaban (uphill). If starting at Halkett Bay, follow the trail (an old logging road) inland and uphill, passing several campsites. After around 40 minutes (1.5 km), you will reach this junction.

2. The Mt. Artaban Trail is marked with orange metal markers. The trail is mostly forested until the peak. It initially travels to the northwest before making a sharp turn to the northeast along the ridge. Some parts of the ridge are steep.

3. The obvious summit has views of Howe Sound and the Vancouver area to the east. The summit used to have a fire lookout tower: built in 1957, it collapsed in the 1970s and its remains were removed around 2011.

Historical Note Mount Artaban was named after Camp Artaban, in Port Graves Bay to your northwest. The camp itself was named after Artaban, the protagonist of *The Other Wise Man* by American author Henry van Dyke.

4. Return the way you came to wherever you're being picked up. (Although it's possible to do a loop by heading north from the peak, the trail is shifting and difficult to follow.)

13. MOUNT GARDNER

Hike to Bowen Island's highest point, and a nearby viewpoint.

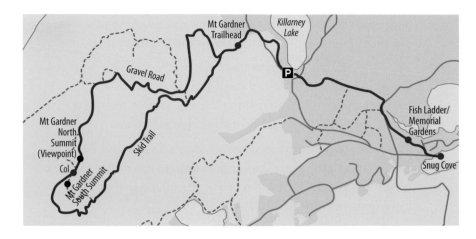

LOCATION

Bowen Island is accessed via BC Ferries from Horseshoe Bay (or private boat). The ferry lands at Snug Cove. It's cheaper to walk from Snug Cove and leave your car at Horseshoe Bay, but you can save 5.8 km (round trip) by driving straight on Bowen Island Trunk Road, turning right on Mt. Gardner Road after 750 m (at the Bowen Island Community School) and then turning left on Bowen Pit Road in 2.2 km. Park along this road and hike uphill to the metal gate, rejoining the trail at step 3.

PUBLIC TRANSIT

Horseshoe Bay is accessed by bus routes #250 and 257 from downtown Vancouver.

DISTANCE

7-km round trip from trailhead, plus 5.8-km round trip hike to trailhead from Snug Cove

ELEVATION GAIN

727 m from Snug Cove

DIFFICULTY
Strenuous (4). Some route finding needed. Steep in sections.

SEASON
Snow-free year-round.

OF SPECIAL INTEREST FOR CHILDREN
There is a radio tower and helicopter landing pad with a good view on the north summit. There is an interesting memorial garden and fish ladders near the start of the hike. The ferry ride adds to the adventure. Shops and restaurants in Snug Cove provide an excellent opportunity for a pre- or post-hike meal, snack or shopping trip. The first 2.9 km (one-way from Snug Cove to the trailhead) could also be biked.

1. From the Snug Cove ferry terminal, turn right (north) on the first road at the library (Cardena Road). After about 100 m, at a sign for Crippen Park, turn left onto a wide gravel trail — follow this trail for 2.5 km to Killarney Lake. You will pass a memorial garden and fish ladders (helping fish return to creeks to spawn) and then cross Miller Road. Turn right (north) on Miller Road, then left (west) on the Killarney Creek Trail in 130 m. After 700 m, turn left (northwest) onto Killarney Creek Trail at a Y-junction.

2. Cross Magee Road; soon you should see Killarney Lake to your right (east).

3. After hiking along the shore of Killarney Lake, you will see a trail to your left (southwest). If you cross a bridge over a swamp, you've gone too far. Take this trail to Mt. Gardner Road; turn right (northwest), then left (southwest) onto Bowen Pit Road. Hike up this road to the metal gate.

4. Continue uphill and then turn left (south) on the marked Skid Trail. After 2 km the trail forks again; go left (southwest) on the marked South Gardner Trail.

5. The South Gardner Trail leads upwards along the side of the mountain. There are several forks. At one fork, the "main" trail seems to go downhill. Don't take this trail; go uphill instead.

Gardner's north summit. Courtesy David Crerar.

6. You will reach another intersection. The trail on your right (north), marked "Mt. Gardner Summits," is the most direct route to the peak but is very steep. Instead, take the South Gardner Trail to your left (south), which wraps around the side of the mountain, passes some viewpoints and leads to the col between Gardner's two summits.

7. Both summit trails are well marked from the col. Most hikers will want to turn left (north) to the north summit, which has a radio tower and helicopter landing pad with a good view of Howe Sound. The south summit is slightly higher but has no view.

The slightly higher, viewless south summit. Courtesy David Crerar.

8. You can return the way you came, or take a more boring (but slightly shorter) gravel road down. Hike north from the north summit, past a large rock; the tree at the start of this trail is flagged with tape. This trail (the Mt. Gardner Trail) is steep in some areas, and ropes are provided. The steepest section is below the peak. This trail leads to a gravel road; turn right (east, downhill) then travel along several switchbacks to the end of Bowen Pit Road.

14. KILLARNEY LAKE

This trail takes you around a peaceful lake on Bowen Island.

LOCATION
Bowen Island is accessed via BC Ferries from Horseshoe Bay. The ferry lands at Snug Cove.

PUBLIC TRANSIT
Horseshoe Bay is accessed by bus routes #250 and 257 from downtown Vancouver.

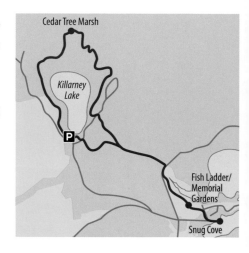

DISTANCE
7.8-km round trip from Snug Cove

ELEVATION GAIN
Minimal

DIFFICULTY
Moderate (3). Flat but long.

SEASON
Snow-free year-round.

OF SPECIAL INTEREST FOR CHILDREN
A scenic lake with a picnic area, an interesting memorial garden and fish ladders can be found near the start of the hike. The ferry ride adds to the adventure. Shops and restaurants in Snug Cove provide an excellent opportunity for a pre- or post-hike meal, snack or shopping trip.

1. From the Snug Cove ferry terminal, turn right on the first road at the library (Cardena Road). After about 100 m, at a sign for Crippen Park, turn left onto a wide gravel trail.

2. You will pass a memorial garden and fish ladders (helping fish return to creeks to spawn) and then cross Miller Road. Turn right (north) on Miller Road, then left (west) on the Killarney

Creek Trail in 130 m. After 700 m, turn left (northwest) onto Killarney Creek Trail at a Y-junction.

3. Cross Magee Road. Soon you should see Killarney Lake to your right (east). There is a bench with a good view of the lake. You will soon pass the parking area, with picnic tables and outhouses.

4. Keep hiking around the lake. You will see another viewpoint in about 10 minutes. Ignore a trail to your left (west), which leads to Mount Gardner (Hike 13). The trail passes over several boardwalks and bridges. At the north end of the lake, a boardwalk leads through a marsh with many dead, eerie-looking cedar trees.

5. Continue around the lake to a gravel road (Magee Road). Turn left (northeast) on the road, then right (southeast) at a gate marked by a green and yellow sign to the ferry. This trail intersects with the Killarney Creek Trail.

6. Continue along the Killarney Creek Trail to Snug Cove.

15. DORMAN POINT

A short, steep hike to a viewpoint
near the Bowen Island ferry terminal.

LOCATION
Bowen Island is accessed via BC Ferries from Horseshoe Bay. The ferry lands at Snug Cove, near the trailhead.

PUBLIC TRANSIT
Horseshoe Bay is accessed by bus routes #250 and 257 from downtown Vancouver.

DISTANCE
2.3-km round trip from Snug Cove

ELEVATION GAIN
110 m

DIFFICULTY
Moderate (3). Short but steep. Exposed bluff at the top means a close eye should be kept on younger or meandering children.

SEASON
Snow-free year-round.

OF SPECIAL INTEREST FOR CHILDREN
There is a viewpoint with arbutus trees and the possibility of spotting bald eagles. There is a beach en route. The ferry ride adds to the adventure. Shops and restaurants in Snug Cove provide an excellent opportunity for a pre- or post-hike meal, snack or shopping trip.

1. Walk off the ferry and head west along Bowen Island Trunk Road. At the crosswalk, turn left and go along the boardwalk. You will pass the Snug Cove beach, worth a stop at low tide. As you enter the forest, you'll see a sign to the Dorman Point Trail to your left.

2. Keep heading uphill (east). The trail becomes a series of switchbacks and then reaches a road — go left. One last steep climb will take you to a rocky bluff with views of Howe Sound and Vancouver.

3. Return the way you came.

Cypress Bowl

16. FOUR LAKES LOOP

This hike takes you past remnants of Hollyburn Mountain's history, including Hollyburn Lodge and historic cabins, while passing four scenic mountain lakes.

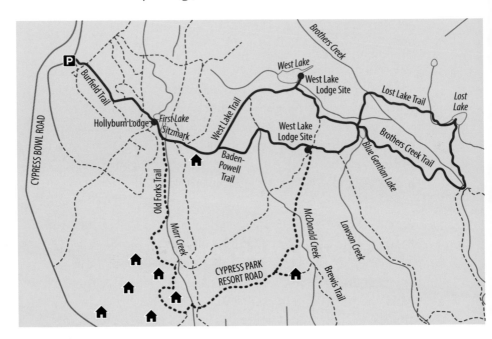

LOCATION

Start from the Cypress Bowl cross-country ski area. From Highway 1, take exit #8 (Cypress Bowl) and turn right at a sign for the cross-country ski area near the top.

PUBLIC TRANSIT

No public transit is available in hiking season.

DISTANCE

7.2-km loop. You can skip Lost Lake for a shorter loop (5 km).

ELEVATION GAIN

100 m

DIFFICULTY
Easy (2). The trail is mostly well defined, but the Lost Lake Trail, although well marked, may be hard to follow in places.

SEASON
Snow-free from early July to October.

OF SPECIAL INTEREST FOR CHILDREN
Old cabins and mountain lakes make this hike worthwhile.

1. Hike up the gravel road next to the info board. Follow the road left (northeast), then turn right on the Burfield Trail (southeast; the first right). After 850 m, you will come to First Lake and the Hollyburn Lodge, which, according to the Hollyburn Ridge Association, was built in 1926–27 by Scandinavian skiers (to replace a 1924 lodge on Hollyburn Ridge). This lodge, and the ski runs built near it, helped to popularize skiing in Vancouver.

2. Continue east on the Sitzmark Trail, along the south shore of First Lake. You will soon join the Baden-Powell Trail; keep going straight (east). The trail passes several cabins, built in the late 1920s and '30s by skiers. Groups of friends or families would choose a site and build a cabin using nearby trees and supplies brought from farther downhill, sometimes learning through trial and error. Over 200 cabins were built; about 100 of them are still standing. According to the Hollyburn Heritage Society, many are privately owned by descendants of the original owners. Please respect owners' privacy.

3. After 500 m, turn left (north) on the West Lake Trail, which leads to the south shore of West Lake. A ski lodge (the West Lake Lodge) stood here from 1928 to 1939, when the building was rebuilt farther south. The new lodge burned down in 1987.

4. Continuing past West Lake, turn left (southeast) at a Y-junction. You will soon reach peaceful Blue Gentian Lake, named after a local flower. There are boardwalks around the lake.

5. Continue east, then southeast, on Brothers Creek Trail along the shore of Blue Gentian Lake. In about 800 m, you will reach a bridge over Brothers Creek. Cross the bridge and head left (north), following signs to Lost Lake, which you will reach in 600 m.

6. Continue west along the Lost Lake Trail to return to Blue Gentian Lake, then keep going southwest past the lake to reach the junction with the Baden-Powell Trail.

7. From here, you can take the direct route (2.4 km) along the Baden-Powell and Burfield trails back to the lodge by turning right (west) on the Baden-Powell Trail. Alternatively, a detour leads past some more cabins (see **Further Adventures** below).

Further Adventures
Visit more cabins along the West Lake Road and Old Forks Trail.

Lost Lake. Courtesy David Crerar.

1. About 150 m after passing Blue Gentian Lake, and turning right on the Baden-Powell Trail, turn left (southwest) on Cypress Park Resort Road, then right (southeast) immediately after. This junction was the site of the West Lake Lodge after it was moved in 1939.

2. Continue southwest along the road. A kilometre past the junction, the Upper Brewis Trail to your left (east) leads to the ruins of an old cabin. When you're done, return to the Cypress Park Resort Road and keep going southwest, past several more cabins. Side trails in the area were built to provide cabin access.

3. Cross Marr Creek and then turn right (northwest) onto another gravel road (Spar Tree Road), which becomes the Old Forks Trail, follows Marr Creek and passes several more cabins. The trail rejoins the Burfield Trail at First Lake.

17. HOLLYBURN MOUNTAIN

The ideal family mountain hike: it's not too far,
it's not too steep and it has a great view!

LOCATION
Start from the Cypress Bowl cross-country ski area. From Highway 1, take exit #8 (Cypress Bowl) and turn right at a sign for the cross-country ski area near the top.

PUBLIC TRANSIT
No public transit is available in hiking season.

DISTANCE
8.2-km round trip

ELEVATION GAIN
410 m

DIFFICULTY
Moderate (3). You're climbing a mountain, but it isn't very steep or far for a mountain.

SEASON
Snow-free from July to October. A snowshoe and cross-country ski trail leads to the summit in the winter.

OF SPECIAL INTEREST FOR CHILDREN
This hike provides beautiful alpine scenery, amazing views and maybe even some blueberries. This is a high-quality hike for relatively little effort.

1. Hike up the gravel road next to the power lines, or head east onto the Sitzmark cross-country trail and then turn left on the Baden-Powell Trail (Wells Gray cross-country trail) for a more scenic route. Wells Gray eventually joins the power line trail.

2. Hike past the Upper Warming Hut onto a clearly defined trail (the Hollyburn Peak Trail). Along this trail, you will see coiled wire buried in the ground, with old wood inside it. These are

Pippa, Isla and Angus on the giraffe tree.

the remains of the old pipes built in the early 1900s to carry water from the mountains to West Vancouver and Vancouver.

3. The trail passes scenic Fourth Lake and then follows the winter trail. There are many blueberry bushes — providing a good snack — from this stretch of trail onward. Bears also enjoy blueberries. If you see one, keep kids near and make a lot of noise.

ABOVE AND FACING PAGE Angus having fun on the peak. Courtesy David Crerar.

4. You will reach a turnoff to the downhill ski area along the Baden-Powell Trail to the left (west). Ignore this trail and keep going straight (north) along the Hollyburn Peak Trail. Kids might like to take breaks and explore several areas along this trail, including a "giraffe tree" that makes a good place to seat kids for a photo, a bench with a good view of Grouse Mountain and its surrounding peaks to the east, and a fallen tree's giant root ball.

5. The switchbacks lead to a beautiful meadow below the peak. Walk past beautiful tarns and tangled trees. The trail climbs upward again to the summit, a large rocky outcrop with excellent views. Whiskey jacks — small gray birds — circle around, trying to steal your lunch. Please don't feed them, as human food is harmful to them and might lead to starvation in the fall and winter when hikers stop visiting the peak in large numbers.

18. BLACK MOUNTAIN AND CABIN LAKE

A trail to a mountain peak with a good view and a scenic lake with salamanders. Bring a bathing suit and towel on a hot day.

LOCATION
Start from the Cypress Bowl downhill ski parking lot. From Highway 1, take exit #8 (Cypress Bowl) and park up the mountain at the end of the road.

PUBLIC TRANSIT
No public transit is available in hiking season.

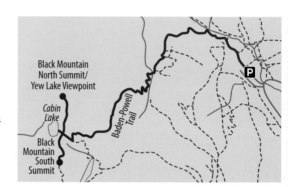

DISTANCE
4.2-km round trip from parking lot

ELEVATION GAIN
300 m

DIFFICULTY
Moderate (3). The trail is steep in places, with some loose rock.

SEASON
Snow-free from July to October. The trail is too steep to hike without microspikes in the winter.

OF SPECIAL INTEREST FOR CHILDREN
There is a good view from the Yew Lake Viewpoint and the summit. Cabin Lake is a great place to swim or look for salamanders.

1. From the parking lot, hike north to the board with a trail map of the Cypress Bowl area. Then take the Baden-Powell Trail south. You will pass a turnoff to the Yew Lake Trail on your right — ignore this trail and go straight (west).

FACING PAGE FROM TOP Swimming in Cabin Lake. Courtesy David Crerar; View of the Lions from the Yew Lake Viewpoint.

2. The wide, gravelly trail is clearly marked as it switchbacks past the ski run. There are some views through the trees.

3. Take a right turn (west) to the Cabin Lake Trail. Soon you will reach Cabin Lake and a T-junction. Look for salamanders in the lake, especially on the rocks near the shore. This is a good place to swim on a hot day before or after reaching the peak.

4. Right (north) from Cabin Lake leads to the Yew Lake Viewpoint, which is also the high point of Black Mountain. Unsurprisingly, it has a good view of Yew Lake, as well as Howe Sound and the Lions. Left (south) from Cabin Lake leads to the Black Mountain summit (although the Yew Lake Viewpoint is slightly higher), with a good view of the city.

Further Adventures
Hike to Eagle Bluffs and Cougar Lake (Hike 19).

19. EAGLE BLUFFS AND COUGAR LAKE

Hike past several alpine lakes to a dramatic viewpoint overlooking the city.

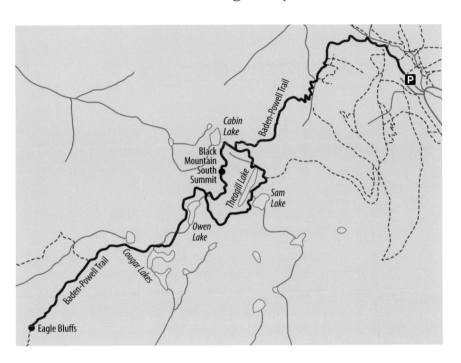

LOCATION
Start from the Cypress Bowl downhill ski parking lot. From Highway 1, take exit #8 (Cypress Bowl) and park up the mountain at the end of the road.

PUBLIC TRANSIT
No public transit is available in hiking season.

DISTANCE
8.2-km round trip to Eagle Bluffs

ELEVATION GAIN
350 m

DIFFICULTY

Strenuous (4). The trail is steep in places, with some loose rock. Lots of elevation gain.

SEASON

Snow-free from July to October. The trail is too steep to hike without microspikes in the winter.

OF SPECIAL INTEREST FOR CHILDREN

The trail passes many scenic lakes, which are fun to explore or rest at, and eventually reaches a bluff with a view.

1. From the parking lot, hike north to the board with a trail map of the Cypress Bowl area. Then take the Baden-Powell Trail south. You will pass a turnoff to the Yew Lake Trail on your right — ignore this trail and go straight (west).

2. The wide, gravelly trail is clearly marked as it switchbacks past the ski run. There are some views through the trees.

3. Ignore a right turn to Cabin Lake and keep going between Theagill (right; west) and Sam (left; east) lakes. Alternatively, take this turn and visit Black Mountain (Hike 18). Hiking south past the summit of Black leads to the Baden-Powell Trail.

4. Hike around Owen Lake on your left, passing through some muddy spots. The Baden-Powell Trail soon reaches a flat area with several small lakes (the Cougar Lakes).

5. After the lakes, the trail steeply descends into a forest before reaching the viewpoint at Eagle Bluffs.

20. YEW LAKE

A short, easy loop around a small mountain lake. The most accessible alpine hike in this book. Note: No dogs allowed.

LOCATION
Start from the Cypress Bowl downhill ski parking lot. From Highway 1, take exit #8 (Cypress Bowl) and park up the mountain at the end of the road.

PUBLIC TRANSIT
No public transit is available in hiking season.

DISTANCE
2.4-km loop

ELEVATION GAIN
25 m

DIFFICULTY
Very easy (1). Well-marked, nontechnical trail with almost no elevation gain. Wheelchair- and stroller-accessible. The Bowen Lookout Trail is moderate (3), because of some steep sections; it is definitely not wheelchair- and stroller-accessible.

SEASON
Snow-free from July to October.

OF SPECIAL INTEREST FOR CHILDREN
The hike offers an easy walk, with a lake and mountain blueberries. There are mushrooms in the fall, especially the rarer boletes and amanitas. Other draws include old-growth trees and picnic tables.

1. From the Cypress Bowl parking lot, hike north past the restaurant, following signs to the Yew Lake Trail. Turn left on the Yew Lake Trail past the trail map. Immediately, you will reach the turnoff for the Howe Sound Crest Trail (HSCT); ignore this trail and go left (west).

2. The trail parallels a creek. There are many blueberry bushes along this trail, providing a quick snack for both humans and black bears. You will reach a turnoff to your right (north) for the Old Growth Loop. This short, worthwhile loop takes you through a bog to a stand of old-growth trees. Watch out for bears.

3. Return to the main trail, which follows the shore of Yew Lake. Several picnic tables make a convenient rest stop. Eventually, the trail follows a creek then joins the Baden-Powell Trail leading back to the parking lot.

Further Adventures

The Bowen Lookout, with a view of Bowen Island, can be reached from the Yew Lake Trail.

1. At the start of the Yew Lake Trail, take the HSCT northwest and uphill. At a water tower, where the HSCT goes right (northwest), go left (west) instead around the tower and along a wide trail. Alternatively, the Old-Growth Loop (step 2) has a connector to this trail.

2. The path turns to the right at a wooden bridge. Keep going uphill through several switchbacks. Turn left at the sign for the Bowen Lookout.

FACING PAGE, CLOCKWISE FROM TOP LEFT Isla setting off on an adventure along the Yew Lake Trail. Courtesy David Crerar; A grade 2 class hikes around Yew Lake. Courtesy David Crerar; View from the Bowen Lookout.

21. ST. MARKS SUMMIT

A challenging yet popular hike to
a viewpoint north of Cypress Bowl.

LOCATION
Start from the Cypress Bowl downhill ski parking lot. From Highway 1, take exit #8 (Cypress Bowl) and park up the mountain at the end of the road.

PUBLIC TRANSIT
No public transit is available in hiking season.

DISTANCE
10.8-km round trip

ELEVATION GAIN
569 m

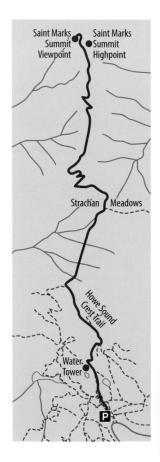

DIFFICULTY
Strenuous (4). Some steep and technical sections and cliffs. This hike is dangerous in the winter.

SEASON
Snow-free from June to October.

OF SPECIAL INTEREST FOR CHILDREN
Much of the trail is along a ridge with views on both sides, adding to the adventure. Viewpoints along the way provide good rest stops. The final viewpoint is a great place for a snack.

1. From the Cypress Bowl parking lot, head toward the ski lodge. Head right (north), past the Olympic rings to the start of the Howe Sound Crest Trail, on which St. Marks is located.

2. The trail continues along a gravel road and ski runs. You will pass a water tower, then enter the forest. Around 1 km into the hike, turn left on a gravel road toward the Lions and Bowen Lookout. Keep going straight as the road becomes a trail, passing a junction with a map and a good view of the Lions.

3. From here, the trail continues north through Strachan Meadows, crossing two small bridges. After the meadow, there is a steep section then the trail flattens out but becomes more technical.

4. Continue along the ridge to a viewpoint with a sign marking St. Marks Summit (the true peak, with almost no views, is at the end of a short trail to the east).

22. MOUNT STRACHAN

An off-the-beaten-path adventure to a very scenic view.
Note: It is pronounced "Strawn," not "Strack-an."

LOCATION
Start from the Cypress Bowl downhill ski parking lot. From Highway 1, take exit #8 (Cypress Bowl) and park up the mountain at the end of the road.

PUBLIC TRANSIT
No public transit is available in hiking season.

DISTANCE
7.2-km round trip

ELEVATION GAIN
500 m

DIFFICULTY
Strenuous (4). Some cliffs. Some route finding needed.

SEASON
Snow-free from June to October. Usually retains snow longer than the rest of Cypress Bowl.

OF SPECIAL INTEREST FOR CHILDREN
The trail is longer and less busy than most Cypress Bowl trails and feels like more of an adventure, especially if you take the Christmas Gully route. Both summits have excellent views and some fun opportunities for scrambling. The trail also passes the site of a plane crash, with a lot of wreckage visible, and a very large old-growth tree. The south summit features several erratics — large boulders carried great distances by retreating glaciers — that are fun to climb, in addition to several sites of striation (large scratches in rocks left by the glaciers).

Debris from a plane crash rests near the trail up Mount Strachan.

1. From the parking lot, follow the Baden-Powell Trail east, away from the peak. After crossing several small streams, turn left (northwest) on a smaller trail heading into the forest (the Old Strachan Trail).

2. You will pass several old-growth trees (including a very large yellow cedar, 3.2 m in diameter, nicknamed the Hollyburn Giant) and a small lake (Emily Lake). The trail plateaus before heading uphill.

3. A very steep section of trail leads to the plane wreckage. You can walk around the debris but please don't touch or disturb the site.

4. The trail eventually leaves the forest and follows the chairlift to the south peak, which has lots of scrambling opportunities.

5. Continue north (downhill) to the col (high point between two peaks) between the north and south summits. The descent can be slippery, so be careful. A trail leads to the north peak, which is slightly higher than the south.

Further Adventures

You can turn this hike into a 10.5-km loop by hiking up or down Christmas Gully on the west side of Strachan. This way requires more route finding and has some steep sections, so its difficulty rating is very strenuous (5). It should only be attempted in dry conditions after all snow has melted.

1. From the parking lot, hike north to the board with a trail map of the Cypress Bowl area and then follow the Howe Sound Crest Trail for about 3 km. You will cross a small bridge and reach Strachan Meadows.

2. Turn right (east) on a faint trail heading uphill along Montizambert Creek. If you've crossed a second small bridge in Strachan Meadows, you've missed the trail.

3. Scramble up the gully (Christmas Gully), along an occasionally marked trail, to the col between Strachan's north and south summits.

FACING PAGE Family pictures on the north and south summits of Mount Strachan. Courtesy David Crerar.

North Vancouver — Capilano Area

23. COHO LOOP AND DAM VIEWPOINT

Hike around the trail circuit in Capilano Canyon, seeing many sights on the way. This was one of the first trails I remember hiking, and it's still a great choice for younger children learning what the forest has to offer.

LOCATION
Park at the Capilano River Hatchery parking lot. From the Upper Levels Highway, take exit #14 (Capilano Road). Drive north on Capilano Road for 1.3 km then turn left on Capilano Park Road (opposite Mt. Crown Road). The parking lot is 1.4 km down this road.

PUBLIC TRANSIT
There is no public transit to the hatchery. The closest public transit access points are:

1. Take bus #232 (from Phibbs Exchange) or #236 (from Lonsdale Quay) to Capilano Road at Clements Avenue. Hike to the Cleveland Dam (Hike 24; see also that hike's **Further Adventures**).

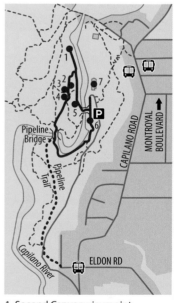

2. Take bus #232, 236 or 247 to Capilano Road at Eldon Road. Take the Pipeline Trail, which starts at the end of Eldon Road and connects to the Coho Loop at the Pipeline Bridge (see step 4 below) 950 m later.

DISTANCE
1.6-km loop

ELEVATION GAIN
76 m

DIFFICULTY
Moderate (3). Some slightly steep sections.

1. Second Canyon viewpoint;
2. Old growth trees; 3. Grandpa Capilano; 4/5. Nurse logs; 6. Cable Pool; 7. Hatchery

SEASON
Year-round

OF SPECIAL INTEREST FOR CHILDREN

The trail starts and ends at a fish hatchery, which has exhibits about salmon in the Capilano River. Many salmon can be seen at the hatchery during spawning season (August to November). The trail itself crosses an impressive wooden bridge and the Pipeline Bridge over the Capilano River. Kids can play on nurse logs along the trail. There is a viewpoint below Cleveland Dam, providing a good view of water rushing down the spillway into Capilano Canyon (especially in spring when more water is released, creating a torrential waterfall). The Pipeline Bridge is fun to cross (don't look down!). There are also plenty of old-growth trees.

1. From the parking lot, hike down the road to the fish hatchery and take the trail opposite the hatchery entrance, crossing a bridge (Cable Pool Bridge) over the Capilano River.

2. At the T-junction past the bridge, turn right (toward the Second Canyon Viewpoint). Follow the canyon (sometimes visible through the trees) north to a viewpoint of Cleveland Dam and Capilano Canyon (try to spot the door in the canyon wall, used for maintenance). Along the trail, an old hollow nurse log acts as a natural playground for kids. Panels at the viewpoint provide information on the dam's history. The viewpoint is colder than the rest of the trail due to mist from the dam, refreshing in the summer but chilly in early spring and winter.

3. Retrace your steps and turn right (west) on the Pipeline Trail right after a small stream. The trail climbs to a plateau with several old-growth trees, including "Grandpa Capilano" (an 800-year-old Douglas fir 2.5 m in diameter). Opposite Grandpa Capilano, kids can walk on a trail along a fallen old-growth nurse log, created by decades of kids doing just that.

4. Past the trees, the trail joins a gravel road then descends to the Pipeline Bridge. Cross the bridge and turn left (southeast) on the Coho Loop at the Y-junction past it.

5. The Coho Loop descends and then ascends as it parallels the canyon. In some places there are views of the opposite canyon rim. Near the end, a left turn (west) marked "Cable Pool" leads to a viewpoint. Steep steps lead down to Cable Pool itself. In spawning season, salmon (and eagles and fishermen trying to catch salmon) can often be found.

6. The loop ends at the hatchery.

Further Adventures

Several trails in the park lead to Cleveland Dam (Hike 24). The two hikes can be combined if you don't mind some extra elevation gain. Refer to that hike's description for route ideas.

FACING PAGE Hikers are dwarfed by one of the many old-growth trees along the Pipeline Trail. Courtesy David Crerar.

24. CLEVELAND DAM/SHINGLEBOLT TRAIL

Cross the Cleveland Dam for a short forest adventure.

LOCATION

Park at Cleveland Park, near the Cleveland Dam. From the Upper Levels Highway, take exit #14 (Capilano Road). Drive north on Capilano Road to Cleveland Park.

PUBLIC TRANSIT

The closest bus stop is Capilano Road at Clements Avenue, accessed by bus routes #232 (from Phibbs Exchange) and #236 (from Lonsdale Quay).

DISTANCE

2.5-km loop, plus 500-m round trip to viewpoint

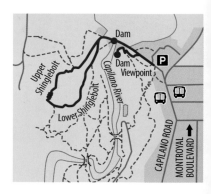

ELEVATION GAIN

52 m

DIFFICULTY

Moderate (3). The Shinglebolt Trail is slippery in wet weather.

SEASON

Year-round

OF SPECIAL INTEREST FOR CHILDREN

The Cleveland Dam has an excellent view of Capilano Canyon, Capilano Lake and the Lions. Kids can also look over the side of the dam to see water leaving the spillway.

1. From the parking lot, hike toward the dam (west). The field near the parking lot has good views of the Lions.

2. Optional viewpoint: Just before the dam, turn left on a somewhat hidden trail leading downhill. Descend several stairs to a viewpoint just below the dam. Return the way you came (or descend to the Coho Loop, Hike 23 – see **Further Adventures**).

FACING PAGE Cleveland Dam, as seen from the viewpoint.

3. Hike along the path over the dam. The Lions and Grouse Mountain are visible to the north — challenge kids to spot the Grouse gondola and chalet — and Capilano Canyon is to the south. Past the dam, the trail forks; go right (uphill) on the Baden-Powell Trail. Just before a bend in the trail, turn onto the Shinglebolt Trail. "Shinglebolt" refers to a block of lumber to be cut into shingles, a throwback to logging in the early 1900s.

4. The trail starts as a wide forest path, then descends a staircase. Where the trail forks, go left (east) on the Lower Shinglebolt Trail. Unlike the Upper Shinglebolt, this trail is not very steep.

5. The Lower Shinglebolt Trail joins the Capilano Pacific Trail near the dam. Keep hiking uphill, cross the dam and return to the parking lot.

Further Adventures

Several trails connect this hike to Hike 23 (Coho Loop and Dam Viewpoint). The easiest is the Capilano Pacific Trail: at the fork on the west side of the dam, head downhill (right) to connect with the Pipeline Trail at the Pipeline Bridge (at step 4 in that hike's trail description).

25. MACKAY CREEK AND BOWSER TRAIL

Neighbourhood creekside hiking trail
with some unexpected history.

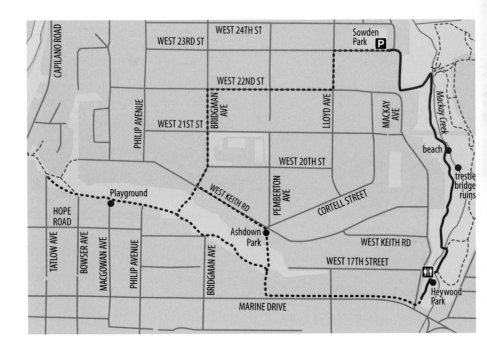

LOCATION
Park at Sowden Park (on 24th Street in Pemberton Heights). Take exit #14 (Capilano Road), turn onto Route 1 East and then turn onto Keith Road to access Pemberton Heights.

PUBLIC TRANSIT
Bus #236 from Lonsdale Quay to Grouse Mountain stops at 22nd Street and Cortell Drive. Keep hiking west on 22nd to reach the entrance to Mackay Creek Park (step 2 below).

DISTANCE
2-km round trip to Heywood Park; 4.2 km including Bowser Trail loop (see **Further Adventures**)

Angus looking for salmon. Courtesy David Crerar.

ELEVATION GAIN
72 m

DIFFICULTY
Easy (2). The trail is well groomed, but there are some steep sections.

SEASON
Year-round

OF SPECIAL INTEREST FOR CHILDREN
The trail follows a creek and has creekside access. Salmon can be seen in Mackay Creek in spawning season. If you're willing to get a bit wet, the ruins of a 1910s trestle bridge can be found in the creek bed; kids will feel like explorers trying to find it.

1. From Sowden Park, hike downhill on a gravel path at the intersection of Mackay Avenue and West 23rd Street (between 2304 and 2306 Mackay). The trail passes the end of a lane before reaching West 22nd Street.

2. At the sign for Heywood Park, turn left and head down a set of stairs into the ravine. Turn right before the bridge.

The remnants of a 1910s trestle bridge.

3. The trail continues along Mackay Creek. There is a boardwalk in one section and some small dirt beaches (look for salmon in the fall). Note the large stumps with axe marks; loggers in the late 1800s and early 1900s would place springboards in these marks for them to stand on while cutting the tree down.

4. The trail suddenly rises. South of this point, the remains of some pilings of a trestle bridge can still be seen in the creek downstream of the first steep uphill section. They're easiest to see in winter, when the view isn't blocked by foliage. In spring or summer, you will need to bushwhack or wade in the creek to see them. With some imagination, kids can picture the old trestle bridge.

Historical Note From 1912 to the late 1940s, a trestle bridge crossed Mackay Creek. The streetcar line ran from the foot of Lonsdale Avenue up Mahon Avenue, crossed Mackay Creek, went along what is now West 21st Street and then turned right on Philip Avenue. The slight turn to the left at the north end of Philip Avenue is a remnant of the streetcar route.

5. The trail has several steep uphills and downhills before crossing the creek. Turn right here and continue to Heywood Park past another bridge.

6. On the way back, you can keep hiking on the east side of the river for a more interesting route (or hike the Bowser Trail; see **Further Adventures #1** below).

Further Adventures #1

The Bowser Trail is a short forest walk leading to another playground and a good view of Vancouver.

1. Turn right on Marine Drive then right on Pemberton Avenue (at the Shell gas station). At the end of Pemberton Avenue, turn left on the Bowser Trail.

2. The Bowser Trail continues along a small creek to Capilano Road. There is a small neighbourhood playground at the end of MacGowan Avenue, roughly two-thirds of the way to Capilano Road. Turn around whenever you want to.

3. There are three steep paths leading up to the Pemberton Heights neighbourhood from the Bowser Trail. Ashdown Park, at the end of Pemberton Avenue, has the best view of Vancouver from the top.

4. From whichever exit you choose, walk to Keith Road, head north on Bridgman Avenue, then turn right on 22nd Street. Turn left on Lloyd Avenue to reach Sowden Park.

Further Adventures #2

If you're feeling very adventurous, you could combine this hike with the Lower Capilano Pacific Trail (Hike 10).

5. From the end of the Bowser Trail, head south on Capilano Road then turn right at the end of Fullerton Avenue.

6. Cross the bridge to Woodcroft and turn left on the stairs past the bridge, which lead to the Lower Capilano Pacific Trail. It's 2.7 km one way from Heywood Park to Woodcroft.

26. LOWER MACKAY CREEK TO KINGS MILL WALK

A pleasant walk along a creek and seawall, with
good views of downtown Vancouver across Burrard Inlet.
Bring your dog, there's a dog park en route.

LOCATION
Park in the southwest parking lot at Capilano Mall. From the
Lions Gate Bridge, go east on Marine Drive, then turn right on
Hamilton Avenue.

PUBLIC TRANSIT
Buses #236, 239, 240, 241, 242, 255 and N24 stop at Capilano
Mall. It might be more convenient to take the SeaBus to Lonsdale
Quay and start hiking from there (hike east/left along the Spirit
Trail to the Burrard Yacht Club and start the loop at step 6).

DISTANCE
3.7-km loop

ELEVATION GAIN
Minimal

DIFFICULTY
Easy (2). High-quality,
flat trail, mostly paved.
The hike crosses 1st
Street.

SEASON
Year-round

**OF SPECIAL INTEREST
FOR CHILDREN**
There are opportunities
to see wildlife, from
salmon in Mackay Creek in the autumn to eagles and herons along
the shore. River otters and beavers are occasionally seen north and
south of 1st Street. The new-ish bridge over the railway is interesting

FROM TOP Kings Mill Walk; A heron at the yacht club.

and has a good view of the shipyards and trains. Interesting bird-house sculptures can be seen along the trail. There is a dog park and volleyball court at Kings Mill Walk. The hike starts and ends at Capilano Mall with many opportunities for a post-hike snack.

1. From Capilano Mall, cross Mackay Creek (there is a bridge just north of the crosswalk near Visions Electronics). Hike down Roosevelt Crescent for 100 m and turn left on the Mackay Creek Trail at the field.

2. The trail follows the creek to 1st Street. This section of Mackay Creek Park was long neglected and used as a dump site until volunteers cleared invasive species and put in native plants from 2015 to 2017. In the fall, keep an eye out for spawning salmon in the creek.

3. Lower Mackay Creek Trail ends at 1st Street. Hike left (east) on the Spirit Trail and cross 1st Street at the intersection.

4. The Spirit Trail continues over the Harbourside West Overpass, built in 2011 to bypass the train tracks. Kids might like to watch the trains below. Past the bridge, head south along the Mackay Creek estuary. There are several bird viewing areas along the trail. Eagles are often found here, especially in autumn (salmon spawning season). There are also several whimsically designed birdhouses.

5. Follow the Spirit Trail past Bodwell High School to the Kings Mill Walk dog park. From here, the trail continues along the seawall. Herons are often found on the rocks in the harbour. There are several picnic tables.

6. At the Burrard Yacht Club, the Spirit Trail heads north. Follow the Spirit Trail to Bewicke Avenue, then follow Bewicke north. Turn left (west) on an unnamed small road at the Mosquito Creek Park sign (just before 2nd Street). Follow a paved path north along Mosquito Creek to Marine Drive.

7. Turn left at Marine Drive and walk two blocks to your car at Capilano Mall.

27. UPPER MOSQUITO CREEK

Hike along Mosquito Creek via a wide gravel trail, with the option of taking a detour on the way back to explore Edgemont Village.

LOCATION
Start at the new Delbrook Community Recreation Centre at Queens Road and Del Rio Drive (William Griffin Park). From the highway, take exit #17 (Westview) and drive north, then turn left on Queens.

PUBLIC TRANSIT
Bus route #232 stops at Del Rio Drive. To avoid retracing your steps, you could catch bus #246 at Montroyal and Skyline at the end of the trail.

DISTANCE
4-km round trip from Delbrook

ELEVATION GAIN
167 m

DIFFICULTY
Moderate (3). Well-marked, steep, gravel trail.

SEASON
Year-round

OF SPECIAL INTEREST FOR CHILDREN
The trail parallels Mosquito Creek and has creek access for most of the hike. Edgemont Village and its shops are nearby.

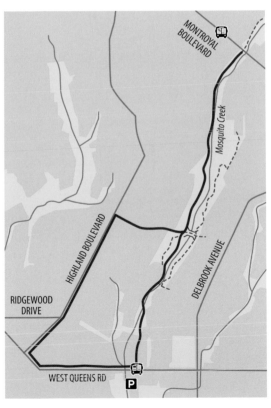

1. Cross Queens Avenue and hike to the end of Del Rio Drive. The trail enters the cedar, fir and hemlock forest and heads uphill.

2. You will pass a bridge with yellow steps. Don't cross it but keep going uphill along the creek.

3. The trail ends at the Montroyal Boulevard bridge. A scary sign warns that the trail ahead is unsafe. Turn around and retrace your steps downhill.

4. At the bridge, with yellow steps, turn right and leave the park. Continue along the road to Highland Boulevard. Turn left. You will reach Edgemont Village, a good opportunity for a snack break.

5. Head south on Edgemont Boulevard then left (east) on Queens to return to your car.

Further Adventures

Keep hiking to Lower Mosquito Creek (Hike 28).

28. LOWER MOSQUITO CREEK

Like the previous hike, this hike follows Mosquito Creek,
this time passing under a bridge and ending at a playground.
The lower section of the creek can also be turned into a loop for
kids eager to explore.

LOCATION
Start at the new Delbrook Community Recreation Centre at Queens Road and Del Rio
Drive. From the highway, take exit #17 (Westview): drive north, then turn left on Queens.

PUBLIC TRANSIT
Bus route #232 stops at Del Rio Drive. To
avoid retracing your steps, you could catch
buses #236, 239, 240, 241, 242, 255 or N24
(at Marine Drive and Fell Avenue), or 249 (at
Bewicke Avenue and Larson Road).

DISTANCE
3.6-km round trip

ELEVATION GAIN
59 m

DIFFICULTY
Moderate (3). Mostly packed gravel on the
west side of the creek. The east side is rougher,
and there's one precarious creek crossing, but
it can be avoided.

SEASON
Year-round

OF SPECIAL INTEREST FOR CHILDREN
The trail parallels Mosquito Creek and has creek access for most of
the hike. There is a playground at Mosquito Creek Park. The trail

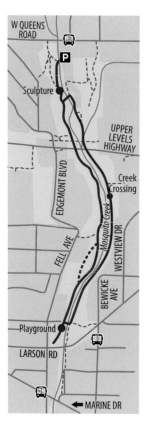

Angus exploring Mosquito Creek. Courtesy David Crerar.

passes under the highway bridge. At one point, the trail crosses a tributary on a narrow plank, adding to the adventure.

1. From Delbrook, hike west on a gravel path past the William Griffin Park sign. The path turns at the skate park and parallels the creek. You will pass the sculpture *Eventually #1*, installed by artist Adam Kuby in 2018. Over time, plants and weather will erode the granite blocks, demonstrating the power of these forces. The other two sculptures in this triptych are located at the Lynn Canyon Cafe (Hike 39) and Maplewood Farm.

2. Continue south through a bigleaf maple forest to the creek. The trail passes under the Upper Levels Highway. Creek access is easy here.

3. Pass two large side trails to your right (leading to Fell Avenue). Another, smaller side trail on your right is an interesting diversion, taking you through a small wetland paralleling the main trail (dogs not allowed).

4. At 17th Street, you will reach fields, a basketball court and a playground. There is also a trail map on the info board.

5. The trail ends at Larson Road, just past the playground, which is a good place for a mid-hike break.

6. On the way back, cross the bridge at the outhouse and turn left at the basketball court onto a trail leading back to Delbrook along Mosquito Creek's east bank. At one point, you cross a tributary on a small wooden plank (this is exciting in the rain!). Some sections may be muddy in rainy weather.

Further Adventures #1
Hike Upper Mosquito Creek (Hike 27).

Further Adventures #2
Capilano Mall is only 650 m from the trail's southern end. Keep walking west (left) along Larson Avenue until it ends at Marine Drive, across from the mall.

29. LONSDALE WATERFRONT

It's not the most "natural" walk, but it offers
great views of the harbour and lots of activities for kids.

LOCATION
Start at the end of Chadwick Court, near the SeaBus terminal. There is a parking garage nearby.

PUBLIC TRANSIT
Take the SeaBus or bus routes #228, 229, 230, 231, 236, 239, 242, 246 or N24 to Lonsdale Quay.

DISTANCE
3.2-km loop

ELEVATION GAIN
Minimal

DIFFICULTY
Easy (2). Paved, mostly flat trail.

SEASON
Year-round

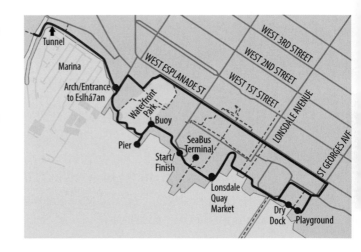

OF SPECIAL INTEREST FOR CHILDREN
There are many things to see on this walk, such as views of Vancouver, herons at the marina, the Lonsdale pier and several sculptures. There are two playgrounds en route. Lonsdale Quay Market is a good place to buy a pre- or post-hike snack. Benches along the seawall make nice rest stops.

1. Hike west on Chadwick Court. Turn left on the Spirit Trail after Chadwick turns and becomes Chesterfield Avenue. Turn left again at the buoy to reach the seawall. You can go to the end of the pier if you like.

Sunset at Lonsdale Quay.

2. Keep going west along the seawall, passing the playground at Waterfront Park, the Sailors Memorial and a display about the Trans Canada Trail. Plaques on the railing provide information about local history. Turn left, under the arch.

3. The Spirit Trail continues through the community of Eslhá7an, on Squamish Nation reserve land, past the Mosquito Creek Marina. At one point, it dips down into a tunnel below sea level to bypass a building. Turn around and retrace your steps at the bridge over Mosquito Creek.

4. At the arch, turn left. Follow the Spirit Trail as it turns right to follow the tracks, but turn left in one block onto a path leading to Esplanade.

5. Go east on Esplanade for 750 m, then turn right on the Spirit Trail at St. Georges Avenue.

6. Continue south along the Spirit Trail to the waterfront. Little kids might enjoy the Shipyards Playground. The Burrard Dry Dock has good views of the city. Once again, there are plaques explaining local history.

7. Continue to Lonsdale Quay Market, maybe buying a snack. Chadwick Court is on the other side of the SeaBus terminal.

Further Adventures
After step 3, you could continue along the Spirit Trail to Kings Mill Walk (Hike 26).

Grouse Area

30. GROUSE MOUNTAIN

A very short hike up a gravel road to a viewpoint.

LOCATION

The trail starts at the top of the Grouse Mountain Skyride (you could combine this hike with the BCMC [BC Mountaineering Club] or Grouse Grind trails, adding another 3 km each way). The Skyride terminal is at the end of Nancy Greene Way in North Vancouver: take exit #14 (Capilano Road) off the Upper Levels Highway and drive north to the end of the road.

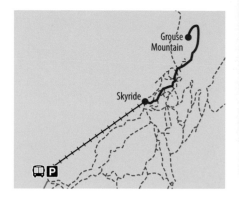

PUBLIC TRANSIT

The Skyride is accessible via bus routes #236 (from Lonsdale Quay) and 232 (from Phibbs Exchange).

DISTANCE

1-km round trip from Skyride

ELEVATION GAIN

140 m

DIFFICULTY

Easy (2). A short hike, but the gravel road may be tiring and/or slippery. A wild grouse (known as Grotius the Grumpy Grouse, or Gregory) has been known to stalk and attack tourists on the summit — do not approach! The Grouse Grind is strenuous (4).

SEASON

Snow-free from June to November.

OF SPECIAL INTEREST FOR CHILDREN

The Skyride adds to the adventure. Grouse Mountain is one of North Vancouver's most-visited tourist attractions, and has

Beware!

many interesting diversions, such as two orphaned grizzly bears, the Lumberjack Show and the Eye of the Wind turbine.

1. From the Skyride, hike east along the paved road, passing the chalet and following the bear paws painted on the path. Turn left at the ski run information board. After several statues, turn left at the next junction.

2. You will pass the Lumberjack Show and arrive at the grizzly bear habitat. If feeling lazy, you can turn left here and take the Peak Chair to the top. If not, keep going past the yurt, pass the Birds in Motion amphitheatre and turn right (uphill).

3. Keep climbing the gravel road to the top of Grouse. You will pass the Eye of the Wind turbine.

Further Adventures

We strongly suggest combining this hike with a hike to Dam Mountain or Thunderbird Ridge (Hikes 31 and 32), or, for more adventurous children, Goat Mountain and/or Goat Ridge (Hikes 33 and 34). All of these hikes are accessed via the Alpine Trail, which starts underneath the Peak Chair.

31. DAM MOUNTAIN

An ideal first mountain hike for beginning hikers and young children. Leads to a peak with good views of Vancouver.

LOCATION
The trail starts from the Grouse Mountain Skyride at the end of Nancy Greene Way in North Vancouver: take exit #14 (Capilano Road) off the Upper Levels Highway and drive north to the end of the road.

PUBLIC TRANSIT
Take bus route #236 (from Lonsdale Quay) or 232 (from Phibbs Exchange) to the Grouse Mountain parking lot.

DISTANCE
4-km round trip from Skyride

ELEVATION GAIN
269 m

DIFFICULTY
Moderate (3). Some slightly steep and rough sections.

SEASON
Snow-free from June to November, and a good snowshoe trail in the winter.

OF SPECIAL INTEREST FOR CHILDREN

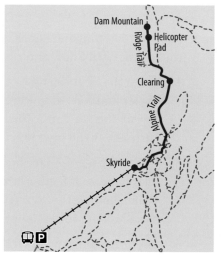

Dam Mountain provides an ideal introduction to hiking for younger children, who can climb a mountain on well-marked trails without venturing too far from civilization. Views of nearby mountains (especially Crown Mountain and the Camel) and the city are a good reward. Younger kids can enjoy sliding down the

FACING PAGE FROM TOP The final ascent of Dam Mountain. Courtesy David Crerar; On a foggy morning, a sentinel guards the peak.

granite slab near the peak. Dam is also a good rest stop on the way to Goat Mountain (Hike 33) or Goat Ridge (Hike 34). There is also a helicopter pad en route.

4. From the chalet, follow bear paws to the bear habitat. Turn left past the yurt, walking along the fence. You will see the Alpine Trail on your right (north), passing underneath the chairlift.

5. Take the Alpine Trail north, around Grouse Mountain. For the first 800 m, the trail is a flat gravel road with views of Capilano Lake (one of the water sources for Greater Vancouver) through the trees.

6. You will reach a small clearing. Turn left (northwest) and begin to climb through the forest. The trail passes under a pipe bringing water from Kennedy Lake to Grouse Mountain Resort, before reaching a Y-junction at a small meadow.

7. Take the Ridge Trail to your left (northwest); the other trail (Alpine Trail) bypasses Dam. The trail passes through two meadows — the second meadow has a helicopter pad that younger children can play on.

8. Hike up a rocky outcrop to the summit.

9. Before leaving, hike a few metres north for a view of Crown Mountain.

Further Adventures
Hike even farther to Thunderbird Ridge (Hike 32) or Goat Mountain (Hike 33) or beyond!

32. THUNDERBIRD RIDGE

*A good side trip from Grouse, Dam or Goat mountain to the end
of a ridge with mountain views.*

LOCATION
Grouse Mountain Skyride (refer to Dam Mountain, Hike 31).

PUBLIC TRANSIT
Take bus route #236 (from
Lonsdale Quay) or 232 (from
Phibbs Exchange) to the
Grouse Mountain parking
lot.

DISTANCE
6-km round trip from chalet;
2-km round-trip detour from
Alpine Trail

ELEVATION GAIN
190 m

DIFFICULTY
Strenuous (4). Some slightly
steep and rough sections.
Cliffs on the ridge proper are easily avoidable.

SEASON
Snow-free from June to November, and a good snowshoe trail in
the winter (follow signs for the Snowshoe Grind).

OF SPECIAL INTEREST FOR CHILDREN
There are views of Greater Vancouver and Kennedy Lake from the
ridge, in addition to all the tourist activities at Grouse Mountain
(see Hike 30).

1. Follow steps 1–3 to Dam Mountain (Hike 31). At the Ridge/
    Alpine junction, turn right (northeast on the Alpine Trail,
    bypassing Dam). Pass a water pipe and the zipline platform

before reaching the Thunderbird Ridge turnoff. (Alternatively, hike to Dam Mountain, keep going along the Ridge Trail and turn right at the T-junction; you will soon arrive at the Thunderbird Trail.)

2. Hike to the northeast along Thunderbird Ridge. The trail descends through mountain blueberries and trees before ascending to the viewpoint at the end of Thunderbird Ridge, with good views of Kennedy Lake (a cirque lake, and the source of Grouse Mountain Resort's water) and the surrounding mountains.

33. GOAT MOUNTAIN

The next step after Dam Mountain: a slightly farther summit with much better views and many granite slabs to play on.

LOCATION
Grouse Mountain Skyride (refer to Dam Mountain, Hike 31).

PUBLIC TRANSIT
Take bus route #236 (from Lonsdale Quay) or 232 (from Phibbs Exchange) to the Grouse Mountain parking lot.

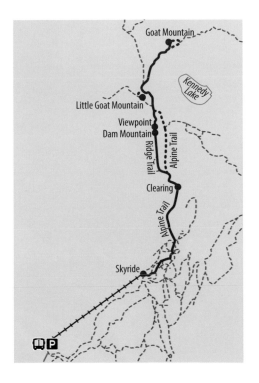

DISTANCE
7-km round trip from chalet; 3-km round trip from Dam Mountain

ELEVATION GAIN
321 m

DIFFICULTY
Strenuous (4) in summer (do not attempt this hike in winter). Some slightly steep and rough sections. Cliffs at the summit — especially to the north — are avoidable.

SEASON
Snow-free from June to November.

OF SPECIAL INTEREST FOR CHILDREN
Good views of the city, and a granite-slab playground, make the peak an excellent spot for a lunch or snack break. Beyond this, Goat Mountain offers kids an opportunity to explore slightly further into the backcountry along well-groomed and marked trails without going anywhere too remote.

FACING/THIS PAGE, CLOCKWISE FROM TOP LEFT A rare sighting at the Alpine/Ridge trail junction. Courtesy David Crerar; Father and son enjoy the view of Crown Mountain and the Camel from Goat. Courtesy David Crerar; The final climb up Goat Mountain. Courtesy David Crerar.

1. Follow directions to Dam Mountain (Hike 31) and keep hiking, or bypass Dam Mountain by turning right on the Alpine Trail at the final junction. The trail is slightly rockier and rootier from here on.

2. The Alpine and Ridge trails merge into one, then diverge again after a few metres. Turn right (northeast) here and hike around Little Goat Mountain.

3. You will reach a T-junction; go right (northeast). (Left leads to Little Goat Mountain, worth the short trip; see **Further Adventures #2**). At the next junction, which is well marked and signposted, turn right (left leads to Crown Mountain, not suitable for younger hikers).

4. The trail takes you along the ridge past a helicopter pad. You will reach a slightly steep area with chains to help if needed (adding to the adventure!).

A little goat on Little Goat. Courtesy David Crerar.

5. Here you can take the short (and very steep) way up, or keep going slightly farther east and turn left (northwest) up a more gradual trail. Both trails lead to the eastern side of the summit. From here it is an obvious hike to the peak.

Further Adventures #1

Continue hiking to Goat Ridge (Hike 34).

Further Adventures #2

Little Goat Mountain is an easy side trip (less than 200 m) from the Goat Mountain Trail. Kids can claim they climbed three mountains instead of two, adding to their sense of accomplishment. It is also usually less crowded than Goat and makes a good picnic spot.

1. At the T-junction mentioned in step 3 above (right before the Crown/Goat junction), turn left toward Little Goat.

2. The trail gently ascends through heather and mountain blueberries. Beware of side trails. You will reach Little Goat in roughly 100 m — the true peak location is a rocky area. A large, axe-marked tree provides shade.

3. Return to the main trail the way you came, or by going past the peak (south)(slightly steeper and longer).

34. GOAT RIDGE

An adventure along a scenic ridge past small lakes to a view of the surrounding mountains. Into the wild!

LOCATION
Grouse Mountain Skyride (refer to Dam Mountain, Hike 31).

PUBLIC TRANSIT
Take bus route #236 (from Lonsdale Quay) or 232 (from Phibbs Exchange) to the Grouse Mountain parking lot.

DISTANCE
10.2-km round trip from chalet; 3-km round trip from Goat Mountain

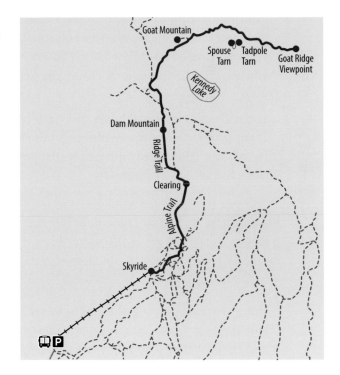

ELEVATION GAIN
371 m

DIFFICULTY
Strenuous (4). Some slightly steep and rough sections. Some route finding might be needed.

SEASON
Snow-free from June to November.

OF SPECIAL INTEREST FOR CHILDREN
Children will feel like explorers on this trail, despite not going anywhere too remote. The ridge trail is an alpine playground,

with many granite slabs — none too steep — to scramble on, and many small trees, creating a very different setting from the rest of the hike. Small lakes along the trail are fun to explore and maybe swim in on a hot day. The viewpoint at the end has an excellent view of most of the Grouse–Goat range, allowing kids to feel accomplished at how much they've done. Blueberry bushes on the trail might be a good snack.

1. Follow steps 1–4 in the previous hike above to Goat Mountain (Hike 33). You can bypass Goat Mountain and continue along the ridge, or visit Goat Mountain and return to this junction. Either way, continue hiking along the ridge.

2. Continue hiking to the end of the ridge along a usually clear trail past mountain blueberries and small trees. In some areas you might need to follow cairns to stay on the path, but if you're going to the end of the ridge, you're going the right way.

3. You will pass two small lakes. The easternmost lake (Tadpole Tarn) is too shallow for swimming, but the westernmost and larger one (the apostrophe-shaped Spouse Tarn) is a nice place to cool off on a hot day.

> **Historical Note** Spouse Tarn is named after Lieutenant John Spouse, who died in the First World War. It was so dedicated by his son, the interestingly named mountaineer Frederic "Brick" Spouse (nicknamed for his red hair).

4. There are two bumps at the end of the ridge. The easternmost and farthest bump has excellent views of the Grouse area and Hanes Valley (the valley immediately to your north). The other bump is the high point but has an inferior view. Its easiest access route is a bushwhack starting from a tarn on the backside.

5. Return the way you came.

FROM TOP Looking toward the end of the ridge in the fog; Spouse Tarn.

North Vancouver — Lynn Valley

35. BIG CEDAR AND KENNEDY FALLS

An adventurous hike to one of the
North Shore's largest old-growth trees,
logging camp remnants and a picturesque waterfall.

LOCATION

From Lynn Valley Road, turn north (uphill) on Mountain Highway. At the end of civilization, you will pass a gate (which closes
at 8:00 pm: beware!). Continue uphill past mountain biking trails
to the Mount Fromme parking lot. (Watch out for bikers!)

PUBLIC TRANSIT

The nearest bus stop is McNair Drive at Tourney Road, accessed
by buses #209 and 210. Hike down McNair Drive, then 950 m up
Mountain Highway to the parking lot.

DISTANCE

7-km round trip to Big Cedar; 10-km round
trip to Kennedy Falls

ELEVATION GAIN

150 m

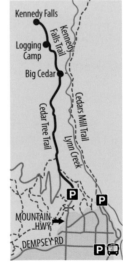

DIFFICULTY

Very strenuous (5). The trail is rough in
places and involves several possibly slippery creek crossings and one descent into
a ravine. At some points you may have to
climb over or around fallen trees, although
this is becoming less of a problem as the
trail becomes more popular.

SEASON

Snow-free except in winter.

OF SPECIAL INTEREST FOR CHILDREN

A massive 600-year-old tree, known as the Big Cedar, and old logging camp remnants will excite imaginative children. For most,

FROM LEFT The Big Cedar; Rusty pieces of metal mark the site of a logging camp. Courtesy David Crerar.

the best reward is the excellent waterfall at the end of the trail, with a small pool that is sometimes (though not often) warm enough for swimming.

1. From the Mount Fromme parking lot, hike north (uphill) along the gravel road, dodging any mountain bikes. The road curves to the northwest. Just before the first switchback (after about 500 m), turn right (north) on the Cedar Tree Trail.

2. Hike along the Cedar Tree Trail, passing the Kirkford mountain bike trail and crossing a wooden bridge over one of many creeks. Although the trail is well marked with yellow markers, you may have to detour over or around fallen trees or

branches. However, as mentioned earlier, these are being cleared more often as the trail becomes more popular. In several areas you will notice the remnants of corduroy roads (a road made from logs placed parallel to one another, commonly used by loggers here in the early 1900s), now part of the trail. Cross several creeks. One crossing near the cedar tree is at the base of a gully and may be tricky.

3. Around the 3.5-km mark, turn a corner and arrive at the unmissable Big Cedar, about 4 m in diameter. It was one of only a few trees not to be logged in the 1920s. Imagine Lynn Valley 150 years ago when most trees looked like this.

4. If continuing to Kennedy Falls, hike uphill to the northwest (behind the tree). Do not take the trail to your right (east), which leads to Lynn Creek.

5. The Kennedy Falls Trail continues northward for another 1.5 km. There are more corduroy roads in this section of the trail, and in one place many pieces of rusty metal uphill from the trail mark the site of an abandoned logging camp. Cross several more creeks and an old landslide before arriving at the obvious final destination. You can scamper down to a rock for a better view, but be careful — it is slippery.

Further Adventures

From the Big Cedar, the trail to your right (east) leads steeply down to Lynn Creek. It is possible to ford Lynn Creek during dry months, walk to a red flag on the other side of the creek and walk inland to the Cedars Mill Trail, leading to an easy and flat 2.8-km hike to the Lynn Headwaters parking lot. However, the 100 m on the east bank between Lynn Creek and the Cedars Mill Trail was very overgrown last time I checked (2018) and required a lot of bushwhacking through prickly growth. Also, do not try to ford Lynn Creek from October to June, or after a heavy rainfall.

36. NORVAN FALLS

*Hike to a beautiful waterfall nestled
in the upper Lynn Creek valley.*

LOCATION

The trail starts from the Lynn Headwaters parking lot, next to the BC Mills House. Travel uphill (northeast, then northwest) on Lynn Valley Road, passing a yellow gate and a sign for Lynn Headwaters. The parking lot is 1.5 km down this road (if it's full, there's an overflow lot 350 m back).

PUBLIC TRANSIT

The closest bus stop is Lynn Valley Road at Dempsey Road, accessible via bus route #228 from Lonsdale Quay.

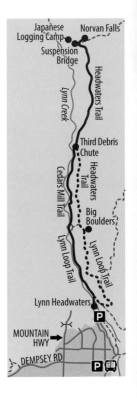

DISTANCE

14 km

ELEVATION GAIN

195 m

DIFFICULTY

Strenuous (4). Flat but long, and soggy when wet (which it often is).

SEASON

Year-round. This is a good hike for spring or winter when higher hikes are still covered in snow.

OF SPECIAL INTEREST FOR CHILDREN

There is a waterfall and remnants from logging days, such as corduroy roads and old machinery. There is also an interesting suspension bridge near the falls.

1. From the parking lot, hike north across a bridge over Lynn Creek. You will see the ruins of a dam that was washed out by heavy rain in the 1980s. Before that, and before the creation

The view from the third debris chute.

of Lynn Headwaters Park, this area was off limits as part of the watershed.

2. Turn left (north) on the Lynn Loop Trail, hiking along the creek. This area was logged in the early 1900s, and remnants from logging days can still be found, such as an old cart and pieces of metal.

3. After 1.9 km, you will reach the junction to Headwaters Trail (see **Further Adventures** below). Go straight (north) along Cedars Mill Trail for 2 km, arriving at a large open area (the third debris chute) with creek access and good views across the valley to Goat Ridge.

4. Keep going north for another 3 km along an old logging road. In some places, the corduroy road (a road made from logs placed parallel to one another) is noticeable underfoot. More leftover logging tools are scattered along the trail. Ignore the turnoff to Coliseum Mountain to your right (northeast). Shortly after this turnoff, you will reach the Norvan Falls turnoff.

ABOVE Crossing the suspension bridge. Courtesy David Crerar.
FACING PAGE Norvan Falls. Courtesy David Crerar.

5. You might want to keep hiking for several metres past the turnoff to the new suspension bridge over Norvan Creek, at the start of the Hanes Valley Trail. Also, remnants of an old (1910s) Japanese logging camp can be seen a few hundred metres along the trail, past the bridge. Once you're done there, retrace your steps and hike uphill to Norvan Falls, visible after a few hundred metres.

6. Return the way you came, or take the Headwaters Trail, which only adds one extra kilometre, though with some elevation gain.

Further Adventures

Take the Headwaters Trail for an interesting loop.

1. At the third debris chute, take Headwaters Trail (left, south-east) instead of the Cedars Mill Trail (right, southwest). This trail parallels the creek farther inland.

2. After 2 km, you can turn right (west) to rejoin the Cedars Mill Trail, or keep going straight (south).

3. If continuing, you will pass some large boulders that make a good rest stop. Pass the Lynn Peak turnoff, then arrive at the connector trail between Lynn Headwaters and the Lower Seymour Conservation Reserve. Turn right (northwest) here; you will rejoin the trail at the Lynn Creek bridge in 0.4 km.

37. LYNN PEAK

A popular, maybe slightly overrated, hike to a viewpoint.
The trail continues to the true summit.

LOCATION
The trail starts from the Lynn Headwaters parking lot, next to the BC Mills House. Travel uphill (northeast) on Lynn Valley Road, passing a yellow gate and a sign for Lynn Headwaters. The parking lot is 1.5 km down this road (if it's full, there is an overflow parking lot 350 m back).

PUBLIC TRANSIT
The closest bus stop is Lynn Valley Road at Dempsey Road, accessible via bus route #228 from Lonsdale Quay.

DISTANCE
8.3-km round trip to Lynn Peak viewpoint; 8.8-km round trip to Rice (South Lynn) Peak; 11.6-km round trip to true Lynn Peak summit

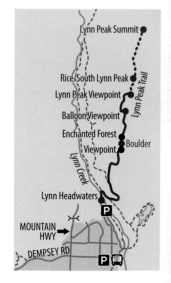

ELEVATION GAIN
720 m to Lynn Peak viewpoint; 801 m to Rice (South Lynn) Peak; 1001 m to true Lynn Peak summit

DIFFICULTY
Strenuous (4). Steep; rocky in places.

SEASON
June to October

OF SPECIAL INTEREST FOR CHILDREN
There are views of the Lower Mainland, plus a grove of old-growth trees. Large boulders (erratics) are fun to climb.

1. From the parking lot, hike north across a bridge over Lynn Creek. Turn right (southeast) toward Rice Lake. You will soon arrive at a junction: turn left (uphill) onto the Lynn Loop

THIS PAGE FROM TOP The balloon used to log Lynn Peak in the 1960s. Courtesy North Vancouver Museum and Archives; While not the true peak, the Lynn Peak Lookout offers the best view, by far, of the adventure.

Trail. After about 800 m, turn right (north) on the Lynn Peak Trail.

2. The trail continues steeply uphill. Around 2 km into the hike, there are limited views of Mount Seymour to the east. You will pass a large boulder, then a grove of old-growth trees known as the Enchanted Forest.

3. About 40 minutes past the first viewpoint, there is a rocky outcrop with good views of Seymour called the Blimp Lookout or Balloon Lookout. Another 40 minutes past the Balloon Lookout, you will reach the Lynn Peak Lookout, with good views of Mount Seymour, Vancouver and the Fraser Valley. For most hikers, this viewpoint is the adventure's highlight.

Historical Note The Blimp Lookout or Balloon Lookout gets its name from a logging company's attempt, in early 1967, to use a large balloon, 41 m by 16 m, to salvage logs felled by 1962's Hurricane Freda. The balloon lasted for three days before drifting to Grouse Mountain and landing on a dead tree. The company tried once more, with a smaller balloon, in October 1967, but again without success.

Further Adventures

The trail continues to the summit of Rice (South Lynn) Peak, then to Lynn Peak itself, both treed summits with little to no view.

1. Continue north along a narrow but well-marked trail. The trail descends and then ascends to Rice Peak (also known as South Lynn Peak), about 500 m past the lookout. The true summit of Rice Peak is a short uphill climb to your left (west) at the root ball of a giant tree. The summit is marked by a small rock pile and a tree with flagging around it.

2. The true Lynn Peak is another 1.4 km farther north. Return to the main Lynn Peak Trail, continue downhill north, then over two small knolls. The trail then rises to a plateau — the summit of Lynn Peak. There is no view. The high point is a granite bump about 30 m off-trail with a cairn.

38. VARLEY TRAIL

A pleasant short walk along Lynn Creek.

> **Historical Note** The trail was named after Group of Seven artist Frederick Varley, who lived at what is now Rice Lake Road from 1932 to 1936 and often walked the route of the Varley Trail.

LOCATION

The trail starts from the end of Rice Lake Road. Drive north on Lynn Valley Road and park near the End of the Line General Store (there is a parking lot one block west of the store, at Kilmer Park on Dempsey Road). Walk across Lynn Valley Road and then north along the road, passing an info board. Turn right on Rice Lake Road 110 m past the End of the Line General Store. The Varley Trail starts at the end of this road.

Alternatively, you could park at the north end of the trail and follow the trail directions in reverse. Travel uphill (northeast) on Lynn Valley Road, passing a yellow gate and a sign for Lynn Headwaters. The Lynn Headwaters parking lot is 1.5 km down this road, next to the BC Mills House (if that lot is full, there is an overflow parking lot 350 m back).

PUBLIC TRANSIT

The closest bus stop is Lynn Valley Road at Dempsey Road, accessible via bus route #228 from Lonsdale Quay.

DISTANCE

3-km round trip

ELEVATION GAIN

33 m

DIFFICULTY

Easy (2). Mostly flat. However, the trail is not stroller-friendly (stairs).

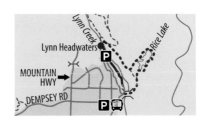

SEASON
Year-round

OF SPECIAL INTEREST FOR CHILDREN
This hike allows for easy access to Lynn Creek. There are salmon-berry-picking opportunities, and the End of the Line General Store has pre- or post-hike snacks.

1. Hike to the end of Rice Lake Road, which becomes Marion Road.

2. The trail follows the west bank of Lynn Creek through the rainforest. Several places offer easy creek access; in the summer, it's nice to soak your feet in the creek while kids play on the banks.

3. You will pass the Lynn Headwaters overflow parking lots before reaching the main Lynn Headwaters parking lot, at the BC Mills House. An info board at Lynn Headwaters has information about the trail's namesake, Frederick Varley.

4. Return the way you came (or keep going; see **Further Adventures #1 and #2** below).

Further Adventures #1
You can access several trails in the Lynn Headwaters area from the northern terminus of the Varley Trail. I recommend a loop via Rice Lake (5.1 km in total, including the Varley Trail).

1. Hike north across a bridge over Lynn Creek. Turn right (southeast) toward Rice Lake. At the junction with the Lynn Loop Trail, keep going straight (southeast).

2. About 900 m later, turn left (north) on the Rice Lake Trail. Follow steps 3–5 of the Rice Lake hike (Hike 40).

3. Once you rejoin the road, hike downhill (southwest) past the gazebo and turn right. The trail leads to the pipe bridge. Cross the bridge to return to Rice Lake Road.

Further Adventures #2

Alternatively, you can hike to Lynn Canyon Park from the Varley Trail's southern terminus at the pipe bridge.

1. From Rice Lake Road, cross the pipe bridge. A trail to your right (south) leads to the 30 Foot Pool (Hike 39).

2. Turn right (west) at a T-junction, then descend several stairs to reach the pool.

39. LYNN CANYON PARK:
30 FOOT POOL AND TWIN FALLS LOOP

Venture beyond the well-known suspension bridge to discover the sights of Lynn Canyon Park, including a scenic waterfall, caves and boulders to explore, plus a swimming hole.

Note Since 1985, 34 people have died from cliff jumping in Lynn Canyon Park, and many more have been injured. Pay attention to the many signs discouraging cliff jumping. Currents and rocks below the surface are usually not visible, and it is very easy to slip on the canyon's algae-covered rocks.

LOCATION

This hike starts from the Lynn Canyon Park parking lot. From the Upper Levels Highway, take exit #19 to Lynn Valley Road. Drive northeast for about 3 km, turning right at the sign for the Lynn Canyon Ecology Centre (Peters Road). The parking lot usually fills up very quickly on weekends and in the summer, so I recommend getting there early or taking public transit.

PUBLIC TRANSIT

The closest bus stop is Peters Road at Duval Road, accessed via bus route #227 from Phibbs Exchange and Lynn Valley Centre. Also, bus 228 stops at Lynn Valley Road and Peters Road, a 1-km walk from the park.

DISTANCE

2.4-km loop

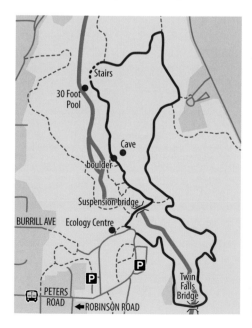

ELEVATION GAIN

122 m

DIFFICULTY

Easy (2). Well-defined, mostly flat trail with some stairs. The suspension bridge might make some kids nervous.

SEASON

Year-round, but more crowded in the summer.

OF SPECIAL INTEREST FOR CHILDREN

The suspension bridge is a fun way to start the hike. Along the trail to the 30 Foot Pool, there is a very small cave that might be fun to explore, and a large boulder that is fun to climb. The 30 Foot Pool is a great place to swim. The trail has a fine view of Twin Falls from the bridge. Finally, the trail starts and ends near the Lynn Canyon Ecology Centre, which is worth the stop and has programs for children.

1. Hike down to the suspension bridge. Try not to look down as you cross; Lynn Creek is 50 m below you.

2. Turn left (northwest) at the T-junction past the bridge. The trail takes you along the river. You will pass a hollowed-out old-growth tree that smaller kids can hide in.

3. The trail passes a large boulder that can be climbed. These boulders, known as "erratics," were carried long distances by glaciers during the ice age and dumped in their current location when the glaciers melted. At the boulder, an unofficial but well-trodden trail leads about 100 m uphill past a swampy area to a small cave (actually the entrance to an old copper mine).

4. Return to the main trail and continue hiking north to the 30 Foot Pool, a beautiful (but usually cold) natural swimming hole.

5. Past the pool, hike up several stairs and turn right (east) then turn right (south) again. Keep hiking south past a turnoff to the suspension bridge (you can return this way and miss Twin Falls if needed).

The 30 Foot Pool. Courtesy David Crerar.

6. Turn right (west) on the Twin Falls Trail and cross the bridge over — unsurprisingly — two waterfalls. Salmon are sometimes seen in the pool below the falls in spawning season (fall), since the falls block them from going any farther.

7. Past the bridge, turn right on the Centennial Trail to return to the parking lot.

Further Adventures
You can combine this hike with Rice Lake (Hike 40) by hiking north past the 30 Foot Pool and then turning right (east) at the pipe bridge (do not cross). Hike uphill to the start of the Seymour Demonstration Forest and Rice Lake Trailhead.

40. RICE LAKE

An easy walk around a lake that used to be one of North Vancouver's sources of drinking water. The hike passes historic log flumes. Note: No dogs are allowed around the lake.

LOCATION
From the Upper Levels High-way, take exit #22A (Mt. Sey-mour Parkway) and drive up Lillooet Road, passing Capilano University and a cemetery. The main parking lot is just past the Seymour–Capilano Water Filtration Plant, with overflow parking just before the plant.

PUBLIC TRANSIT
The closest bus stop on Lillooet Road is 3.8 km away at Cap-ilano University; it's faster and safer to take bus #227 to Lynn Canyon Park (Hike 39) and walk from there (refer to that route's trail description).

DISTANCE
3-km loop

ELEVATION GAIN
Minimal

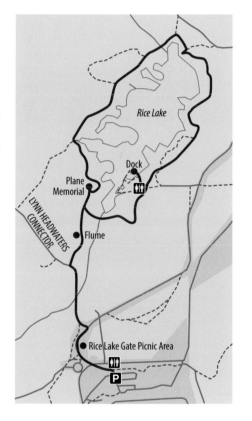

DIFFICULTY
Easy (2). Well-maintained and marked trail. Wheelchair- and stroller-friendly.

SEASON
Year-round. The rainforest around the lake provides some cover from rain.

OF SPECIAL INTEREST FOR CHILDREN

The trail follows the lakeshore and provides many places to explore or rest. There is also a reconstructed log flume (used to transport logs).

1. From the parking lot, hike west past the outhouse and through two gates to the picnic area at Rice Lake Gate. Across the road, a gravel path leads north to Rice Lake.

2. Walk along this path and turn right (north) through a gate. On your left is a restored log flume, used to transport logs from the forests above Rice Lake down to Burrard Inlet.

3. The next junction marks the start of the loop. Go left here. You'll pass a memorial to the victims of a 1947 plane crash.

> **Historical Note** In 1947, Trans Canada Air Lines Flight 3, a Lockheed Lodestar, was on its way from Lethbridge, Alberta, to Vancouver when it crashed on the remote slopes of Mount Elsay to your north. The three crew members and 12 passengers aboard all perished. Its location was a mystery for many years before it was discovered in 1994 by local hikers.

4. Continue clockwise around the loop, passing several lake viewpoints and benches. The best viewpoint is a bridge to a small island near the end of the loop. This bridge and its adjacent dock are good places for a snack or lunch break.

5. Rejoin the trail back to the parking lot.

41. HASTINGS CREEK PARK

*A little-known neighbourhood trail following the small creek
that flows through central Lynn Valley upstream.*

LOCATION

The southern trailhead is a small (unmarked) gravel parking lot
on Hoskins Road, about 50 m north of the intersection with
Arborlynn Drive. From the Upper Levels Highway, take exit #21
(Arborlynn Drive) if heading northwest; or, if heading southeast,
take exit #19 (Lynn Valley Road) and turn right on Kirkstone
Road, then right on Arborlynn.

PUBLIC TRANSIT

The closest bus stop is Hoskins Road at Greenock Place, accessed
via bus route #227 (the trailhead is across the bridge).

DISTANCE

2.8-km round trip

ELEVATION GAIN

71 m

DIFFICULTY

Moderate (3). Some muddy and
rooty sections. Lots of elevation
changes.

SEASON

Year-round

OF SPECIAL INTEREST
FOR CHILDREN

Kids might like to explore the
creek and its mini-beaches. Boardwalks and wooden stairs add to
the adventure. Younger kids will
like the playground at Ross Road
Elementary School, near the end of the trail.

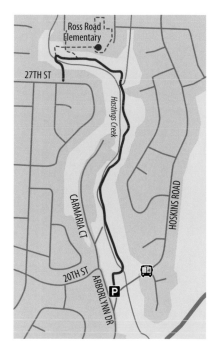

1. From the parking lot, hike north into the forest.

2. The trail follows Hastings Creek. There are boardwalks and stairs in several places. Some parts of the trail are at creek level, and some are farther uphill.

3. The trail passes Ross Road Elementary School (its playground is a good post-hike reward for younger children), crosses the creek and ends at 27th Street. Return the way you came or catch a nearby bus.

FROM LEFT A banana slug at Hastings Creek Park. Courtesy David Crerar; Exploring Hastings Creek. Courtesy David Crerar.

42. FISHERMAN'S TRAIL

A historic, peaceful walk along the Seymour River.

LOCATION

The Fisherman's Trail starts at the northern end of Riverside Drive, but only residents can park there from May to September. The closest public parking lot during those months is at the end of Hyannis Drive. From there, take the Baden-Powell Trail west (downhill) to the Fisherman's trailhead.

PUBLIC TRANSIT

The closest bus stop is Berkeley Avenue at Hyannis Drive, a block away from the Baden-Powell connector. Take bus #214 from Phibbs Exchange, then turn left (northwest) on Hyannis to access the Baden-Powell Trail. Riverside Drive is not accessible via public transit.

DISTANCE

5.8-km round trip from Riverside Drive; the Baden-Powell connector is an extra 1.5-km round trip

ELEVATION GAIN

Minimal along Fisherman's Trail. The Baden-Powell connector adds 82 m.

DIFFICULTY

Easy (2). Mostly flat, wide trail.

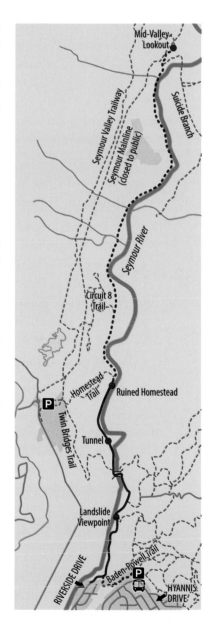

SEASON
Year-round

OF SPECIAL INTEREST FOR CHILDREN
This trail used to be a logging road, so it's a good route for a family biking trip, or for kids to ride bikes while parents jog. The trail parallels Seymour River in many places and has good views of a 2014 rock slide. The new suspension bridge over the Seymour River is interesting. The trail also has several remnants of forgotten history, such as the ruins of old homesteads and (probably the most interesting attraction) a tunnel through the rock, built for a water pipeline.

1. From the parking lot at the end of Hyannis Drive, take the Baden-Powell Trail downhill (southwest), then turn right (north) on the Fisherman's Trail just before Riverside Drive.

2. After about 1 km, just before the junction with the Bridle Trail, the trail passes a viewpoint and information board for a 2014 rock slide that sent over 50,000 cubic metres of rock into the Seymour River. This slide closed several trails temporarily and raised the water level. It also blocked salmon from spawning upstream, forcing volunteers to transport fish over the slide until a restoration project was finished in July 2019.

3. Cross the Seymour River suspension bridge, the fourth bridge on this site.

Historical Note After crossing the bridge, you will pass a trail heading uphill to your left (west). This trail's confusing name, Twin Bridges Trail, comes from the fact that there formerly were two bridges here, constructed in 1908 and 1926 respectively. These twin bridges were removed in 1992 and 2008, and a concrete span was completed in 2009. Barely five years later, the still-new concrete structure was damaged by the 2014 rock slide and ensuing flood and was replaced in 2018.

4. The Fisherman's Trail follows the river north, passing through a gate. On your left, the trail passes a short tunnel built in

A view of the landslide that temporarily dammed the Seymour River in 2014. Courtesy David Crerar.

1907 for a water pipeline. Bring a flashlight and walk through the tunnel if you like. A panel gives some information about the tunnel and the logging industry. Below the panel is a pool in the river where loggers floated shinglebolts (blocks of lumber to be cut into shingles).

5. Hiking north from the tunnel, several small side trails to your right (east) lead to the ruins of old homesteads, such as concrete foundations and chimneys. A mossy wooden arch marks the site of one of the most accessible homesteads.

6. At the junction with the Homestead Trail, return the way you came (or keep going; see **Further Adventures**).

Further Adventures #1

The Fisherman's Trail continues north for another 5 km to the Mid-Valley Lookout, with picnic tables and a good view of the Fannin Range (the mountains behind Mount Seymour, including Mount Elsay). On very rare occasions, mountain goats can be seen on the peaks to the west (the Needles). Keep heading north, past the Homestead Trail. There are some narrow sections over landslide debris. A bike is recommended here to save time. Note: Dogs are not allowed past the Homestead Trail junction.

Further Adventures #2

The Twin Bridges and Homestead trails lead uphill to the Rice Lake parking lot (see Hike 40), so this hike can be combined with trails in that area.

FACING PAGE FROM TOP The entrance to the tunnel is hidden by large ferns. Courtesy David Crerar; Angus explores the ruined doorway of an old homestead. Courtesy David Crerar.

43. MAPLEWOOD FLATS

A stroller- and wheelchair-accessible shoreline and forest walk through a conservation area teeming with wildlife.

LOCATION
The trail starts at the Wild Bird Trust of BC (WBT) office at 2645 Dollarton Highway. From Highway 1, take exit #23B (Dollarton Highway), then turn right after about 1.5 km, just before the Pacific Environmental Science Centre.

PUBLIC TRANSIT
The closest bus stop is along the 2500-block of Dollarton Highway, which can be reached via buses #212 and 215 from Phibbs Exchange.

DISTANCE
2.4-km loop

ELEVATION GAIN
Minimal

DIFFICULTY
Very easy (1). Flat and stroller-friendly.

SEASON
Year-round

OF SPECIAL INTEREST FOR CHILDREN
The park is home to many species of birds, which could be a great scavenger hunt for

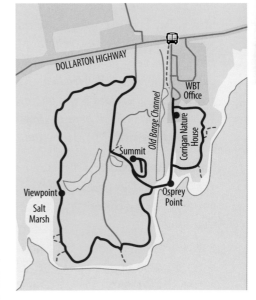

younger kids: see who can spot the most birds. The trail has various viewpoints over Burrard Inlet. Several replica shacks depict the history of this area. There are blackberry bushes along the trail. At very low tides, you can visit a sandbar, usually hidden underwater.

The (muddy) beach at Maplewood Flats. Courtesy David Crerar.

1. Hike south from the WBT office. Near the office are several replica shacks constructed by Vancouver artist Ken Lum.

> **Historical Note** From the 1940s to 1971, a community of hippies and artists lived in Maplewood Flats in shacks like the ones recreated by Ken Lum, until they were forcibly evicted and their shacks burned. The author Malcolm Lowry lived in a similar community at Cates Park (see Hike 44) in the 1940s, and one of the sculptures here is a replica of his shack. Eventually, the conservation area was created in the 1980s.

2. At Osprey Point, to the left (south) just before the bridge, there is a beach with good views of Burrard Inlet. At very low tides (rare), it is possible to walk three-quarters of the way into Burrard Inlet via a sandbar. Cross Old Barge Channel.

A view of Burnaby across Burrard Inlet. Courtesy David Crerar.

3. Turn left (south) at the fork immediately past the bridge. The trail passes several shoreline viewpoints, some with benches. At the southwestern corner of the park, the trail turns northward, passing a viewpoint for a salt marsh and a pond with plenty of waterfowl. After returning to the forest, you'll see several blackberry bushes along the trail — a good snack in blackberry season.

4. The trail loops around the western half of the park, joining a service road. Turn left (east) on a trail between two ponds. At the next junction, the left trail leads to a treed summit that used to have a view. Return to the main trail and cross the bridge again.

5. Past the bridge, a trail on your right (east) leads to another, smaller loop with views of the mud flats before returning to the parking lot.

44. CATES PARK/WHEY-AH-WICHEN

*This waterfront park has many trails to explore
along the shoreline, one of which leads to the
ruins of a 1920s lumber mill.*

LOCATION
Park at the east end of the lower parking lot (near the Cates Park
Paddling Centre). From Highway 1, take exit #23B (Dollarton
Highway) then turn right on Cates Park Road in about 5 km.

PUBLIC TRANSIT
The closest bus stop is along the 4000-block of Dollarton Highway, which can be reached by bus #212 from Phibbs Exchange.

DISTANCE
1.5-km loop

ELEVATION GAIN
Minimal

DIFFICULTY
Very easy (1).
Flat and
stroller-friendly.

SEASON
Year-round

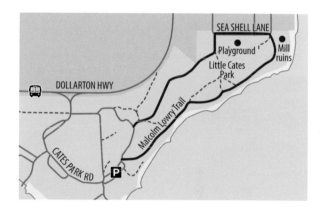

OF SPECIAL INTEREST FOR CHILDREN
There are many beachcombing opportunities along the shoreline,
especially in the tidal pools. Challenge kids to find as many species — or interesting things — as they can. The concrete ruins of
a lumber mill burner are fun for younger kids to play in. The park
also has playgrounds, fields and a concession stand.

1. From the parking lot, hike east along the shoreline. Several
    staircases along the trail lead to the beach. The area was home
    to its own community of squatters from the 1930s until 1958
    when their shacks were destroyed. This trail (the Malcolm

Lowry Trail) was named after the famous English novelist, who lived here in the 1940s.

2. At a Y-junction, turn right (southeast) to continue walking along the shoreline. This trail leads to Little Cates Park, with its own field and playground.

Historical Note Little Cates Park was the site of a lumber mill built in 1916 by American businessman Robert Dollar. The mill stopped operating in 1929, and all that remains is the concrete base of a waste burner (near the playground) that makes a great fort for kids to play in.

3. Hike west along Sea Shell Lane. The trail continues westward through the forest to the upper parking lot at Cates Park.

Playing on the beach at Cates Park. Courtesy David Crerar.

Seymour Area

45. GOLDIE LAKE LOOP

An easy walk to a mountain lake through scenic alpine forest.

LOCATION
The Mount Seymour parking lot at the end of Mt. Seymour Road.

PUBLIC TRANSIT
There is no public transit up the mountain in hiking season. The closest bus stop is Mt. Seymour Road at Mt. Seymour Parkway, 9 km downhill (at Parkgate Mall, serviced by bus route #215 from Phibbs Exchange).

DISTANCE
4-km loop

ELEVATION GAIN
100 m

DIFFICULTY
Easy (2). Some elevation gain. Well-marked trail.

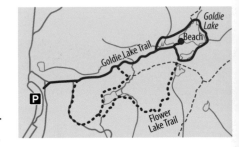

SEASON
Snow-free from June to November.

OF SPECIAL INTEREST FOR CHILDREN
The lures of this hike include an easily accessible lake, blueberries and mushrooms in the autumn.

1. From the Mount Seymour parking lot, walk to the Goldie Lake rope tow and hike downhill (east), past the magic carpet.

2. The trail soon enters the forest. There are many blueberry bushes here, providing a good snack for parents, though kids may find them too sour. You will reach the junction for the Flower Lake Loop; turn left (northeast) to continue on the Goldie Lake Trail.

3. The trail comes to a second junction. Turn left again, starting the loop around Goldie Lake itself, which you will soon see at a viewpoint.

Exploring one of several lakes along the Goldie Lake Trail. Courtesy David Crerar.

An arm of Goldie Lake. Courtesy David Crerar.

4. The trail loops around Goldie Lake, climbing a small hill and crossing a bridge over a stream. There are several nice places for a lunch or snack break, especially a grassy beach with several rocks to sit on (turn right/north at the first junction past the bridge).

5. Return the way you came or via the Flower Lake Trail (see **Further Adventures** below).

Further Adventures

Continue your adventure along Flower Lake Trail.

1. From the beach, walk south to the junction with Flower Lake Trail and turn left (east).

2. The trail passes a small lake before reaching Flower Lake on your right. You can hike to the parking lot from here along the ski run, or loop back to the Goldie Lake Trail and hike back from there.

46. DINKEY PEAK

A very easy hike to a very dinky peak.
It makes a nice loop with First Lake Trail.

LOCATION
The Mount Seymour parking lot at the end of Mt. Seymour Road.

PUBLIC TRANSIT
There is no public transit up the mountain in hiking season. The closest bus stop is Mt. Seymour Road at Mt. Seymour Parkway, 9 km downhill (at Parkgate Mall, serviced by bus route #215 from Phibbs Exchange).

DISTANCE
0.6-km round trip

ELEVATION GAIN
46 m

DIFFICULTY
Easy (2). Short with one steep section.

SEASON
Snow-free from June to November.

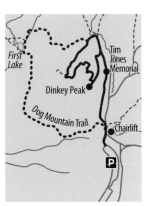

OF SPECIAL INTEREST FOR CHILDREN
The hike is very short and has some views.

1. From the north end of the Mount Seymour parking lot, hike north past the Mystery chairlift. Turn left (north) on the Mount Seymour Trail, which runs parallel to the ski run (the trail west leads to Dog Mountain, Hike 47). You will pass a memorial to North Shore Rescue team leader Tim Jones, well known for promoting NSR and assisting in hundreds of rescues. In 2014, he died of a heart attack while returning from the NSR cabin on Mount Seymour.

2. Soon you'll see and hear the small dam to the right, below.

3. After about 500 m, turn left on the trail to the Dinkey Peak Lookout. There are good views of the parking lot below you,

as well as the Lower Mainland. It's a fun place to run around and explore, but be careful of the steep slopes around.

4. Continue west and up to the true Dinkey Peak for views of Pump Peak (northeast), Cathedral Mountain (northwest; the second-highest North Shore peak), and the North Shore Rescue Cabin, Suicide Bluffs and Brunswick Mountain (west; the highest North Shore peak).

5. Continue down and north along the loop trail to a signpost, and then north and east to rejoin the Mount Seymour Trail.

FACING PAGE Angus and Nana taking the final steps toward mighty Dinkey Peak. Courtesy David Crerar.
ABOVE Exploring First Lake on a cold October morning. Courtesy David Crerar.

Further Adventures

At the signpost, turn left (west) on First Lake Trail to hike down a rooty and at times wet and muddy trail to First Lake. From there, you can add 2 km to go to and from Dog Mountain (Hike 47), or else head back to the start of the Dog Lake hike, at the parking lot.

47. DOG MOUNTAIN

*Hike past lakes to an often-Instagrammed viewpoint
over the Lower Mainland.*

LOCATION

The Mount Seymour parking lot at the end of Mt. Seymour Road.

PUBLIC TRANSIT

There is no public transit up the mountain in hiking season. The
closest bus stop is Mt. Seymour Road at Mt. Seymour Parkway,
9 km downhill (at Parkgate Mall, serviced by bus route #215 from
Phibbs Exchange).

DISTANCE
4.4-km round
trip

**ELEVATION
GAIN**
34 m

DIFFICULTY
Moderate (3).
Relatively flat
and short, but
there are some
technical sec-
tions of trail.
Watch out for
cliffs, aggres-
sive ravens and

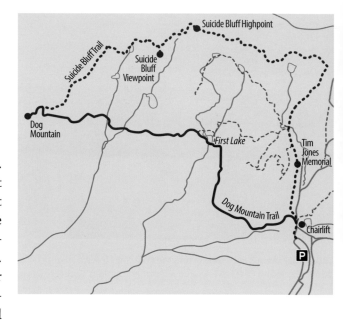

tourists at the peak. The Suicide Bluffs route (see **Further Adventures** below) is very strenuous (5) due to several very steep sections and cliffs.

SEASON

Snow-free from June to November. A good snowshoe trail in the
winter.

OF SPECIAL INTEREST FOR CHILDREN

This hike involves an easy trail with mountain lakes and good views. You will also see some huge ravens.

1. Hike north from the Mount Seymour parking lot. Just past the chairlift, turn left (west) on the Dog Mountain Trail.

2. The trail is easy to follow but has rooty and rocky sections. After about 900 m, start going uphill, then downhill, and you will reach scenic First Lake, a good spot for a snack or lunch break. After First Lake, ignore the Dinkey Peak Trail to your right and keep going west on the Dog Mountain Trail.

3. You will pass two small ponds and then reach a Y-junction. The more defined trail to your left (west) leads to Dog Mountain (right leads to Suicide Bluffs). Go left.

4. The trail soon emerges onto the rocky viewpoint.

Further Adventures

Families looking for more adventure can return via Suicide Bluffs to the northeast of Dog. This rugged trail has several steep sections and cliffs that should be avoided, but the views are better and the trail will be much less crowded.

1. After returning to the forest, turn left (north) on a defined yet unofficial trail; a metal tag on a tree is marked "Suicide Bluffs Trail."

2. The trail passes five small lakes (tarns) before reaching a great viewpoint. Descend then ascend again to the high point; some ropes are provided if needed. The high point has good views of the Seymour area and Seymour River. Avoid the sheer cliffs to the north.

3. The trail continues eastward, over another small knoll, then descends again. You will see the rope marking the Mount Seymour ski area boundary. The trail rejoins the Mount Seymour trail; head right (downhill) to the parking lot.

48. MYSTERY LAKE

Hike to a beautiful alpine lake with
many salamanders to be found.

LOCATION
The Mount Seymour parking lot at the end of Mt. Seymour Road.

PUBLIC TRANSIT
There is no public transit up the mountain in hiking season. The closest bus stop is Mt. Seymour Road at Mt. Seymour Parkway, 9 km downhill (at Parkgate Mall, serviced by bus route #215 from Phibbs Exchange).

DISTANCE
3-km round trip

ELEVATION GAIN
150 m

DIFFICULTY
Moderate (3). Short but some sections are steep or technical.

SEASON
Snow-free from June to early November.

OF SPECIAL INTEREST FOR CHILDREN
The lake is a nice lunch spot and a good place to cool off on a hot day. Salamanders can often be found in the lake.

1. From the north end of the Mount Seymour parking lot, head north to the chairlift. Just past the chairlift, a marked trail leads right (east) into the forest and uphill.

2. Follow this trail uphill and to the northeast. There are many blueberry bushes along the trail that will probably be delicious for adults, though kids may find them slightly sour.

3. You will reach Mystery Lake after 1 km. Take a break here and look for salamanders from the island in the centre (named Salamander Island).

FROM TOP Looking for salamanders; One of many salamander larvae in Mystery Lake.

4. Return the way you came (or keep going; see **Further Adventures** below).

Further Adventures

Continue along the trail to de Pencier Bluffs and/or Pump Peak, Tim Jones Peak and Mount Seymour.

49. DE PENCIER BLUFFS

A short hike to a good view of Indian Arm.
Less well marked but also less crowded than Dog Mountain.

LOCATION
The Mount Seymour parking lot at the end of Mt. Seymour Road.

PUBLIC TRANSIT
There is no public transit up the mountain in hiking season. The closest bus stop is Mt. Seymour Road at Mt. Seymour Parkway, 9 km downhill (at Parkgate Mall, serviced by bus route #215 from Phibbs Exchange).

DISTANCE
5-km round trip

ELEVATION GAIN
200 m

DIFFICULTY
Moderate (3). Some route finding needed.

SEASON
Snow-free from June to November.

OF SPECIAL INTEREST FOR CHILDREN
There is a good view of Indian Arm and the Lower Mainland. There are also blueberries on hand, with leaves that turn

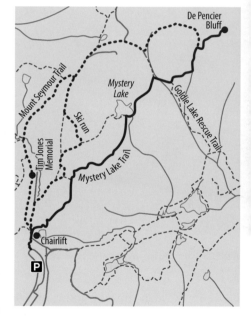

brilliant scarlet in autumn. This hike provides plenty of opportunities to explore.

Historical Note The bluffs were named after Reverend Adam de Pencier, the third Anglican bishop of New Westminster.

A thermal inversion – a rare weather phenomenon involving a layer of fog near the ground – viewed from the De Pencier summit plateau. Courtesy David Crerar.

1. Hike to Mystery Lake (Hike 48).

2. A trail follows the eastern shore of Mystery Lake before heading northeast over rocky bluffs. Take this trail over several small bluffs and past several small lakes.

3. The trail reaches a small creek. When hiking along this creek, you will see the Brockton chairlift to your left (northwest) along the main trail. Instead of walking toward the chairlift,

turn right (and slightly behind you) along a faint trail. This next portion may be overgrown, particularly in late summer. Use a map: the trail is marked on Gaia and OpenStreetMap.

4. Go downhill, cross a creek and continue straight for a portion. Descend into a small valley. *Do not* keep hiking down the southward steep and overgrown rescue trail to Goldie Lake. Instead, go uphill and east. The trail is usually flagged and there is a small sign for De Pencier Bluffs.

5. Go up, down to another area with lots of small lakes, then up again. Just before the crest, a trail (usually but not always marked) leads up to the right (east). Take this trail.

6. You will reach an open area with boulders and a viewpoint to your right. Go left (uphill) along a faint but obvious trail.

7. The trail goes through several swampy areas and rock slabs to reach the flat summit. The high point is in a grove of trees.

ALTERNATE ROUTE

This route is slightly easier than the other one, but it's longer and less interesting, following a ski run for most of the way. You could make a loop and return this way.

1. From the parking lot, take the Mount Seymour gravel trail. At a direction sign, just before the main trail dips down to a small lake, continue on the gravel road right (east) and up, toward the Mystery Peak chairlift. You will come to a signpost under the chairlift. A faint trail continues east to de Pencier. It goes briefly uphill, downhill past a few small tarns and then through a meadowy area with a few more tarns.

2. At this point, the trail is clearer and leads to a straight southbound trail. Go a few paces downhill: it will take you to the side trail (see above) up to de Pencier.

50. PUMP PEAK/TIM JONES PEAK/MOUNT SEYMOUR

A scenic hike to three peaks with increasingly superb views.

LOCATION
The Mount Seymour parking lot at the end of Mt. Seymour Road.

PUBLIC TRANSIT
There is no public transit up the mountain in hiking season. The closest bus stop is Mt. Seymour Road at Mt. Seymour Parkway, 9 km downhill (at Parkgate Mall, serviced by bus route #215 from Phibbs Exchange).

DISTANCE
5-km round trip to Pump Peak; 6-km round trip to Tim Jones; 6.8-km round trip to Seymour

ELEVATION GAIN
400 m to Pump; 500 m to Tim Jones; 660 m to Seymour

DIFFICULTY
Moderate (3) to Pump; strenuous (4) to Tim Jones and Seymour (in good weather). Watch out for snow lingering into springtime, and cliffs. North Shore Rescue has rescued many hikers from the Mount Seymour area, although this may be partly due to the hike's popularity. There are some steep sections of trail between Tim Jones and Seymour.

SEASON
Snow-free from late June/early July to November. The hike is less crowded, and has fewer bugs, in September and October.

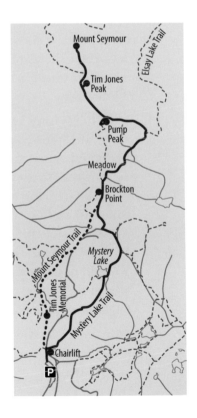

ABOVE Pump Peak as viewed from Brockton Point.
FACING PAGE The approach to Pump Peak. Courtesy David Crerar.

OF SPECIAL INTEREST FOR CHILDREN

Kids will feel like kings after climbing any of the three summits, with excellent views of the entire Lower Mainland. Since the hike has three peaks, it is very flexible — keep going if kids want more, or cut the hike short at Pump or Tim Jones in bad weather. Varied scenery (from forest to lakeside to bluffs to peaks) makes the hike more interesting.

1. Hike to Mystery Lake (Hike 48). A trail follows the eastern shore of Mystery Lake before heading northeast over rocky bluffs. Take this trail over several small bluffs and past many small lakes. You will see the Brockton chairlift to your left (northwest) along the main trail. Continue along the chairlift to join the Mount Seymour Trail at Brockton Point. (Note: A more direct, yet boring, route involves hiking along the Mount Seymour Trail, a gravel road parallel to the ski run. You will pass a memorial to Tim Jones [see below]. At a flat area of the ski run, turn left [down] toward a small tarn [the Sugar Bowl], then take the trail up to Brockton Point.)

2. From Brockton Point, follow the trail northeast toward Pump Peak. The trail descends to a meadow before ascending again around the base of Pump Peak. Do not take the Elsay Lake trail to your east.

3. The trail climbs to the west along rocky slabs. You will reach a gateway with a small tarn and a good view of Pump Peak; the peak is an easy scramble from here. A wooden marker (that reads "First Peak") marks the summit.

Historical Note Pump Peak received its name in 1908 after mountaineers from the BC Mountaineering Club thought that a group of trees on the summit (now long gone) looked like an old pump.

4. Return to the Mount Seymour Trail, visible from the peak, and keep heading northwest along granite slabs that are fun to scramble over. The route is marked by cairns and paint. The trail descends, then ascends to the Tim Jones turnoff. Turn right (east) and you will soon reach Tim Jones Peak, named after the former North Shore Rescue team leader, well known for promoting NSR and assisting in hundreds of rescues. In 2014, he died of a heart attack while returning from the NSR cabin on Mount Seymour. There is a memorial to him along the trail at the site.

5. Retrace your steps from Tim Jones Peak to the Mount Seymour Trail. Descend a very steep section before ascending to the peak of Mount Seymour. Enjoy the views.

6. Return the way you came.

FACING PAGE The final scramble up Pump Peak, with Mount Seymour in the background. Courtesy David Crerar.

APPENDIX: "BEST OF" LISTS

Not sure where to hike? Here are some curated lists of hikes, sorted by category. The best hikes in each category are at the top of each list.

Difficulty/Age

Best hikes for newbies/under-5s

Short hikes with a reward at the end. All these hikes are stroller-friendly.

- Cates Park/Whey-ah-wichen (Hike 44)
- West Vancouver Waterfront (Hike 9)
- Maplewood Flats (Hike 43)
- Lower Mackay Creek to Kings Mill Walk (Hike 26)
- Dinkey Peak (Hike 46)

Best hikes for teens and tweens ready for more

Everyone's stamina and comfort zones are different, but these hikes are longer and more adventurous than most in this book.

- Big Cedar and Kennedy Falls (Hike 35)
- Suicide Bluffs (a **Further Adventure** from Dog Mountain, Hike 47)
- Goat Ridge (Hike 34)
- Norvan Falls (Hike 36)
- Pump Peak/Tim Jones Peak/Mount Seymour (Hike 50)
- Tunnel Bluffs (Hike 1)

Best hikes for kids in wheelchairs or on crutches to enjoy nature

- Yew Lake (Hike 20)
- Maplewood Flats (Hike 43)
- Lower Mackay Creek to Kings Mill Walk (Hike 26)

- Lower Mosquito Creek (Hike 28)
- Rice Lake (not wheelchair-accessible but doable with crutches) (Hike 40)
- Coho Loop and Dam Viewpoint (not wheelchair-accessible but doable with crutches if the child is reasonably fit and strong) (Hike 23)

Season

Best rainy day hikes

These are mostly forested and not too long.

- Coho Loop and Dam Viewpoint (Hike 23)
- Rice Lake (Hike 40)
- Lynn Canyon Park (Hike 39)
- Yew Lake (Hike 20)
- Fisherman's Trail (Hike 42)
- Mackay Creek and Bowser Trail (Hike 25)
- Lower Mosquito Creek (Hike 28)
- Upper Mosquito Creek (Hike 27)
- Goldie Lake Loop (Hike 45)

Best hikes for shoulder season

These hikes are still very enjoyable when hikes farther uphill are covered in snow.

- Lighthouse Park (Hike 5)
- Cleveland Dam/Shinglebolt Trail, and Coho Loop and Dam Viewpoint (Hikes 24 and 23, respectively)
- Lynn Canyon Park (Hike 39)
- Big Cedar and Kennedy Falls (Hike 35)
- Norvan Falls (Hike 36)

- Rice Lake (Hike 40)
- Lower Mackay Creek to Kings Mill Walk (Hike 26)
- Cates Park/Whey-ah-wichen (Hike 44)
- Killarney Lake (Hike 14)
- Fisherman's Trail (Hike 42)

Best winter hikes

These are good snowshoe trips but be sure to check avalanche reports at avalanche.ca first.

- Hollyburn Mountain (Hike 17)
- Dog Mountain (Hike 47)
- Thunderbird Ridge (Hike 32)
- Dam Mountain (Hike 31)
- Dinkey Peak (Hike 46)

Scenery/Destinations

Best campsites

These are good places to camp. Note: Camping is not allowed in some places (such as Bowen Island). Check local regulations before camping.

- Black Mountain and Cabin Lake (Hike 18): camp on the south summit or at Cabin Lake
- Mount Artaban (Hike 12): camp at Halkett Bay
- De Pencier Bluffs (Hike 49): camp on the summit
- Hollyburn Mountain (Hike 17): camp on the summit

Best waterfalls

Based on various factors, including accessibility, height, consistency and the quality of the view (Is it obscured by trees? Is the viewpoint near the falls at the right angle?), that combine for an overall "impressiveness" ranking.

- Kennedy Falls (Hike 35)
- Twin Falls (Lynn Canyon Park, Hike 39)
- Norvan Falls (Hike 36)
- Lower Cypress Falls (Hike 6)
- Upper Cypress Falls (Hike 6)
- Brothers Creek Falls (Brothers Creek Heritage Walk, Hike 8)

Most historical

These hikes have something to teach us about local history. The list prioritizes hikes with historical artifacts (e.g., Brothers Creek Heritage Walk) over hikes with just plaques (e.g., Lonsdale waterfront), since kids will probably find them more interesting.

- Brothers Creek Heritage Walk (Hike 8): logging ruins
- Lawson Creek Forestry Heritage Walk (Hike 7): logging ruins
- Mount Strachan (Hike 22): plane crash
- Fisherman's Trail (Hike 42): homesteads
- Norvan Falls (Hike 36): logging ruins
- Big Cedar and Kennedy Falls (Hike 35): logging ruins
- Cates Park/Whey-ah-wichen (Hike 44): old mill
- Lighthouse Park (Hike 5): lighthouse, old cabins
- Rice Lake (Hike 40): old flume, plane crash memorial
- Lynn Canyon Park (Hike 39): suspension bridge and mine
- Maplewood Flats (Hike 43): shack replicas

Best places to spot wildlife

These hikes give you the best chance to see wildlife in the wild, especially in the early morning or later afternoon. Salmon spawn in the fall (August–November; varies by creek and species), attracting predators such as eagles and bears. I've ranked them by the probability of seeing wildlife. Note that this is inversely proportional to the awesomeness of said wildlife (bears are much more interesting than salamanders but rarely seen). Finally, although it can be irresistible at times, remember not to feed wildlife. It can make them sick and dependent on human food.

- Maplewood Flats (Hike 43): various birds
- Mystery Lake, and Pump Peak/Tim Jones Peak/Mount Seymour (Hikes 48 and 50, respectively): salamanders
- Black Mountain and Cabin Lake (Hike 18): salamanders, whiskey jacks, bears
- Lighthouse Park (Hike 5): various birds
- Coho Loop and Dam Viewpoint (Hike 23): eagles, salmon
- Lower Mackay Creek to Kings Mill Walk (Hike 26): eagles, herons, beavers, river otters
- Lower Capilano Pacific Trail (Hike 10): eagles
- West Vancouver Waterfront (Hike 9): otters, herons and other birds
- Hollyburn Mountain (Hike 17): bears, whiskey jacks
- Black Mountain and Cabin Lake (Hike 18): bears, whiskey jacks
- Mount Strachan (Hike 22): bears, whiskey jacks

Best beaches
These are peaceful places to relax and/or explore.

- Whytecliff Park (Hike 2)
- Starboat Cove (Lighthouse Park, Hike 5)
- West Beach (Lighthouse Park, Hike 5)
- East Beach (Lighthouse Park, Hike 5)
- Dundarave Beach (West Vancouver Waterfront, Hike 9)
- Ambleside Beach (West Vancouver Waterfront, Hike 9)
- Cates Park/Whey-ah-wichen (Hike 44)
- Maplewood Flats (Hike 43)

Other

Best adventures

These hikes will make your kids feel like explorers. They involve venturing into the wild and have many interesting things to discover (ancient trees, remnants of history) and/or factors adding to the adventure (a water taxi, rickety suspension bridges, etc.).

- Goat Ridge (Hike 34)
- Mount Killam (Hike 11)
- Mount Artaban (Hike 12)
- Big Cedar and Kennedy Falls (Hike 35)
- Mount Strachan (Hike 22)
- Lynn Canyon Park (Hike 39)
- Tunnel Bluffs (Hike 1)
- Mount Gardner (Hike 13)
- Pump Peak/Tim Jones Peak/Mount Seymour (Hike 50)
- Hollyburn Mountain (Hike 17)
- Goat Mountain (Hike 33)
- Brothers Creek Heritage Walk (Hike 8)
- Lawson Creek Forestry Heritage Walk (Hike 7)

Best bike trails

These are bike-friendly, mostly flat and don't involve crossing too many roads.

- Fisherman's Trail (to Mid-Valley Lookout) (Hike 42)
- Killarney Lake (Hike 14)
- Lower Capilano Pacific Trail (Hike 10)
- Lower Mackay Creek to Kings Mill Walk (Hike 26)

Best hikes for friends from out of town

These hikes offer adventures, sights and experiences that are harder to find outside of Vancouver.

- Lynn Canyon Park (cross the suspension bridge) (Hike 39)
- Big Cedar and Kennedy Falls (Hike 35)
- Mount Artaban (Hike 12)
- Lighthouse Park (Hike 5)
- Goat Mountain (Hike 33)
- Goat Ridge (Hike 34)
- Brothers Creek Heritage Walk (Hike 8)
- Lawson Creek Forestry Heritage Walk (Hike 7)

ACKNOWLEDGEMENTS

I'd like to thank my parents for taking me on many hikes from a young age. I consider myself extremely lucky to have had the opportunity to discover so much of the North Shore and experience so many incredible adventures. I'd also like to thank the North Vancouver Museum and Archives for some of the historical information (and one of the photos) used in this book, as well as David Crerar for his photos. Finally, I'd like to thank Pippa, Isla and Angus Crerar, who always inspire me to keep exploring.

Harrison Crerar grew up exploring the trails, creeks and mountains of his hometown, North Vancouver. With three younger siblings, he has lots of experience hiking with kids of all ages on many different trails. He is also an avid runner, and loves travel and adventures, whether hiking, on skis or in a kayak or canoe. With David Crerar and Bill Maurer, he is the co-author of *The Glorious Mountains of Vancouver's North Shore* (RMB, 2018). He is currently studying biology at McGill University.

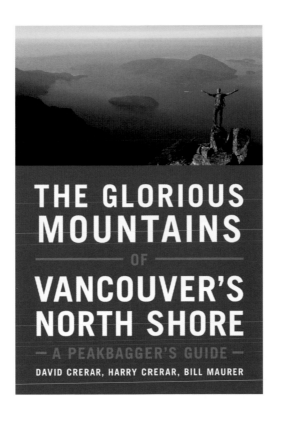

The Glorious Mountains
of Vancouver's North Shore

A Peakbagger's Guide

DAVID CRERAR, HARRY CRERAR, BILL MAURER

9781771602419

Family Walks and Hikes of Vancouver Island

Volume 1

Victoria to Nanaimo

THEO DOMBROWSKI

9781771602792

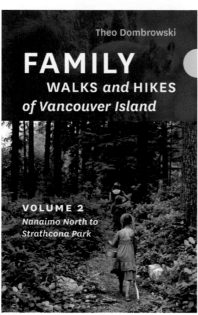

Family Walks and Hikes of Vancouver Island

Volume 2

Nanaimo to Strathcona Park

THEO DOMBROWSKI

9781771602815

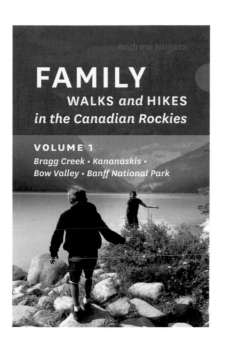

Family Walks and Hikes of the Canadian Rockies

Volume 1

Bragg Creek - Kananaskis - Bow Valley - Banff National Park

ANDREW NUGARA

9781771602242

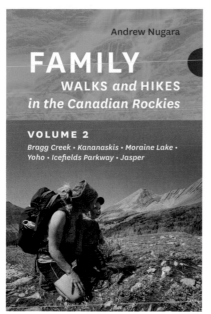

Family Walks and Hikes of the Canadian Rockies

Volume 2

Bragg Creek – Kananaskis – Moraine Lake – Yoho – Icefields Parkway – Jasper

ANDREW NUGARA

9781771603058